99

THE LOW CARB
NUTRiBULLET
RECIPE BOOK

205 Delicious & Nutritious Recipes

Revised Second Edition published by Reciprocity in 2015
All rights reserved

WRITERS
Marco Black & Oliver Lahoud

ILLUSTRATOR
David Joyce

Disclaimer
The information in this book is provided on the basis that neither the authors nor the editors nor the publishers shall have any responsibility for any loss or damage that results or is claimed to have resulted from reading it. Some of the recipes contain nuts or nut milk. If you have a nut allergy please avoid those particular recipes.

CONTENTS

The Low Carb Smoothie Recipe Book
All recipes have 20 carb grams or less

Superfood Double Fruit Blasts - *Made entirely out of Superfoods*

Superfood Double Fruit Smoothies - *Made entirely out of Superfoods*

Superfood Fruit and Veggie Blasts - *Made entirely out of Superfoods*

Superfood Fruit and Veggie Smoothies - *Made entirely out of Superfoods*

Heart Care Double Fruit Blasts
Anti-inflammatory, high in Omega 3, anti oxidants, Vitamins C, E

Heart Care Fruit & Veggie Blasts
Anti-inflammatory, high in Omega 3, anti oxidants, Vitamins C, E

Happiness, Deep Sleep and Stress Busting Blasts
High in Tryptophan, Magnesium,. Vits B3, B6, B9

Detoxing and Cleansing Smoothies
All ingredients have detoxing capabilities

Clear Thinking Brain Food Blasts - *High in Omega3, Beta Carotene, Lycopene, Magnesium, Zinc, Vitamins B, C, E*

Radiant Skin Nourishing Blasts
High in Anti oxidants, Caroteinoids, Polyphenols, Pectin, Zinc, Vitamins A, C

Radiant Skin Nourishing Smoothies
High in Anti oxidants, Caroteinoids, Polyphenols, Pectin, Zinc, Vitamins A, C

Dessert Blasts - *Yummy*

THE LOW CARB NUTRiBULLET RECIPE BOOK

Classic Low Carb Blasts - *All less than 20 Carb grams*

Classic Low Carb Smoothies - *All less than 20 Carb grams*

Classic Low Carb Blasts with Flavour Boosts - *All less than 20 Carb grams*

Classic Low Carb Smoothies with Flavour Boosts
All less than 20 Carb grams

The Low Carb Smoothie Recipe Book
All recipes have 20 carb grams or less

The Lower the Carbs the Better the Health

The view until a few years ago was that saturated fat was bad for your heart, bad for your arteries and caused weight gain. This view was based upon the premise that "You are what you eat." So it seemed logical to believe that if you ate fat you would get fat.

However the human body is not a passive recipient of food. If you eat a hamburger you do not become a hamburger. The body metabolises everything that we eat. So we are not what we eat at all. We are, in fact, what the body makes out of what we eat. Putting this another way..

"We are what we eat – metabolised"

The supermarket shelves are full of low fat foods. These were supposed to make us all thinner. But the truth is that in the West, the average person is getting fatter not thinner. Yes fat contains 9 kcal per gram whereas protein and carbohydrate contain only 4 kcal per gram. So again it seemed logical to deduce that cutting down on fat would makes us thinner and healthier. Many people today religiously cut all the fat off their meat before consumption. It's a noble effort. But we now know, from bitter experience, that it is doomed to failure. Nature provides whole foods for a reason. And we should eat what is provided whole as much as possible. For fat is an apetite suppressor and it is not the villain of the obesity epidemic. It was merely the most obvious suspect.

Carb, carbs, carbs are the disaster. And every supermarket is full of them. Our food shops are a sea of carbohydrate. That is why we are getting fatter and fatter. And that is why 30% of people over 60 in the West are diabetic. We are overloading our carb metabolisms from day one. When you eat too much carb and do not burn it off, you stress our your pancreas and become ill. When you eat too much fat you do not. Eskimos have been eating no carbs for hundreds of years – because you cannot grow much wheat in the arctic. They used to have no diabetes at all until they started eating cookies and sitting about in front of computers rather than catching fish and building igloos.

The even more counter intuitive result of the latest dietary research is that high carb diets cause cardio vascular disease and arterial sclerosis not fats. Eating more fat and therefore less carb actually improves your blood lipids (blood fats such as cholesterol). The writer was diabetic and now eats an ultra low carb diet with an enormous amount of saturated fat. Initially he thought that this would make him into a heart attack waiting to happen. But his cholesterol levels have only improved the more fat and the less carbs that he has eaten!

So the moral of the story is that a little knowledge is a dangerous thing. Two stage thinking is what is required here not one stage thinking. Because the body is a complex and brilliant mechanism. It is not passive. It is active. If you push it in one direction, it will react and push back in the other.

The Health Benefits of Smoothie Raw Vegetable Variation

Many clinical studies have shown that raw vegetables help fight the big killers today. They help significantly to fight Cancer (the more veggies and the less meat you eat the better your body can prevent and fight tumours). There was a wonderful study done on the Norwegians during the second world war when the German occupiers commandeered all their meat. The result was that the incidence of all types of cancer in Norwegians fell by more than 50%.

They help fight Cardio Vascular Disease. They provide essential antioxidants, oils, minerals, vitamins and are generally better for us than a hamburger or a pork sausage. But the trouble is that they normally do not taste as good as a hamburger or a pork sausage unless they are roasted with cheese or boiled to the point where they have lost most of their goodness.

This is where the high power blender comes in. It makes veggies taste great. A smoothie can taste as good and as invigorating as a steak with fries or a cappuccino with a croissant or a chocolate torte with cream. Your mother would never have had to tell you to: "Eat your Greens" had your family possessed a high power blender and a good recipe book.

The manufacturers claim all sorts of health benefits from it. And without going into medical detail, whatever the goodness is in a vegetable or leafy green or fruit or nut or seed, the high power blender can get that goodness out without destroying the delicate biochemical compounds with heat from cooking them. It is billed not as a blender or a juicer, but as an extractor. This is because the machine represents the best method mankind presently has of extracting the goodness from non meat food. The blades break down the cell walls of the ingredients and thereby release the cell contents into your intestines. So unless you have teeth which can rotate at 10,000 rpm, the modern blender represents a significant advance on chewing.

The other psychological trait of mankind which works against us here, is that we are loyal to what we like. Most of retail commerce is based upon brand loyalty. Although this type of loyalty doesn't always work so well with romantic partners! So we find a vegetable we like and then just eat that all the time. I mean once I have a record that I like, I will listen to it over and over again. So even if we do eat some vegetables or leafy greens or fruits, they will tend to be repetitions of a very small selection of what is available. They will just the ones that we have become familiar with and grown to like. They are essentially the vegetable next door.

So the purpose of this book is to empower to reader to vary their vegetables and fruits and greens and nuts and seeds on a daily basis. That is why we have included so many delicious Blasts and Smoothies. If you only drink a small fraction of these smoothie recipes you will be deficient in nothing that nature provides from Vegetables, Fruits, Nuts, Seeds and Greens.

Certain amino acids (protein) and fatty acids (fat) vitamins and minerals cannot be manufactured by the body. So they have to be eaten. This is one of the reasons why food variation is so important. Failing to eat certain essential foods can be lethal – even if you are putting on weight from all the food that you are eating! This was discovered when canned liquid diets were first invented. Some of the people who tried these out for more than a month just dropped dead due to running out of essential amino acids.

Essential Amino Acids

There are 11 of them: Tryptophan, Tyrosine, Threonine, Isoleucine, Histidine Leucine, Lysine, Methionine, Phenylaneline, Cysteine and Valine. These are nicely distributed throughout the leafy greens and although meat and dairy have more protein and therefore more essential amino acids than greens per gram they have less protein than green per kcal. So for dieters, Spinach (yummy) and Kale (if you can stand it) are a good option.

One 200 ml glass of whole milk has between 22-38% of the Recommended Daily Intake of all of the 11 essential amino acids (except Cysteine – 14% of the RDI). We use 200 ml of whole milk in some of our Blast and Smoothie Recipes.

Essential Vitamins

These are: A, B1 (Thiamin), B2 (Riboflavin), B3 (Niacin), B4 (Choline/Adenine)) B5 (Pantotheic Acid), B6 (Pyridoxines), B7 (Biotin)B9 (Folates), B12 (Cobalamin), C, D3, E, K

Stop Press: The latest EU guidelines for Vitamin D3 are now 4000 IU per day rather than 400! Also the latest research shows that high dose Vitamin D3 toxicity is caused by a lack of Vitamin K2. Spinach and Kale are rich in K1 which the body can convert into K2. But 100 micrograms of K2 supplementation (MK7 variety) is recommended for each 1000 IU of Vitamin D3. Vitamin K2 is expensive so eat your dark leafy greens!

Essential Oils and Fats

This is a very short list. Basically the more fish based Omega3 (EPA DHA in particular) the better up to around 5 grams per day. And the more seed nut or vegetable based Omega3 (ALA) the better without limit.

There is plenty of evidence that Omega 3 in your diet has a large effect upon the cardio vascular system. In particular the Omega3 fish based or vegetable and seed based fatty acids should be eaten in larger amounts if you are on a high fat diet. There are good Omega3 supplements out there but whole foods containing Omega3 normally provide better absorption into the body than Omega3 supplements.

The 10 Essential Minerals

Calcium, Copper, Iron, Magnesium, Manganese, Phosphours, Potassium, Selenium, Sodium, Zinc

25 Widely Recognized Superfoods

These Superfoods contain many of the essential amino acids, fats, vitamins and minerals. But that is not why they are superfoods. They are defined as superfoods due to the health benefits that they confer. They are generally rich in anthocyanins, polyphenols, flavenoids, antioxidants, cancer fighting ellagic acid, heart disease fighting lycopene and other really useful nutrients which whilst not essential (in the sense that they can be manufactured by the body if it has the right components to hand), promote good health, fitness and well being. Between them these Superfoods are attributed with the following health benefits…

Increased Protection from Bacterial and Viral Infections
Increased Immune Function
Reduced Cancer Risk
Protection Against Heart Disease
Slowing Aging
DNA Repair and Protection
Prevention and reduction of Cardiovascular Disease
Reduced Hypertension (High Blood Pressure)
Alzheimer's Protection
Osteoporosis Protection
Stroke Prevention
Reduced Risk of Colon Cancer

Protection Against Heart Disease
Antioxidant Protection
Prevention of Epileptic Seizures
Prevention of Alopecia (Spot Baldness)
Reduced Risk of Type II Diabetes
Reduced Frequency of Migraine Headaches
Alleviation of Premenstrual Syndrome (PMS)
Regulation of Blood Sugar and Insulin Dependence
Slowing the progression of AIDS
Protection Against Dementia
Improved Eye Health
Alleviation of Inflammation
Alleviation of the Common Cold
Improving Sleep depth and length
Detoxing and Cleasning the body
Improving Bones Teeth Nerves and Muscle

Buckwheat and **Quinoa**: Too high in carbs to be included in our list and not suitable for a Blender Recipe

Chili Peppers and Garlic: Great but not really suitable for a Blender Recipe

Almonds: High in Protein, unsaturated Fat, Vitamins B1, B2, B3, B9, E, Calcium, Copper, Iron, Magnesium Phosphorus, Potassium, Zinc and Fibre

Dark Cholcolate: High in Protein, Saturated Fat, Vitamins B1, B2, B3, B9, K, Calcium, Copper, Magnesium Manganese, Phosphorus, Potassium, Selenium, Zinc and Fibre

Flax Seeds: High in Protein, unsaturated Fat, Vitamins B1, B3, B5, B6, B9, Calcium, Copper, Iron, Magnesium, Manganese, Phosphorus, Potassium, Selenium, Zinc, Fibre

Pumpkin Seeds: High in Protein,unsaturated Fat, Vitamins B2, B3, B5, B6, B9, E, Calcium, Copper, Iron, Magnesium, Manganese, Phosphorus, Potassium, Selenium, Zinc

Chia Seeds: High in Protein, has all essential amino acids in good quantity, incredibly high in Fibre at 34%, High in Omega3 at 17%, Vitamins B1, B2, B3, B9, Calcium, Copper Manganese, Phosphorus, Selenium, Zinc

Apricots: High in Vitamins A.C, E, Iron, Potassium, Fibre

Avocados: High in unsaturated Fat, Vitamins B2, B3, B5, B6, B9, C, K Cooper, Magnesium, Manganese and Potassium, Fibre

Blueberries: High in Vitamins B9, C, K, Manganese and Fibre

Raspberries: High in Vitamins B1, B2, B3, B9, C, K, Copper, Iron, Manganese and Fibre

Blackberries: High in Vitamins B9, C, K, Manganese and Fibre

Guavas: High in Vitamins: A, B9, C, Copper, Magnesium, Manganese, Potassium, Fibre

Papaya: High in Vitamins A, B9, C, Potassium, Fiber

Goji Berries: Contains all 11 Essential amino Acids - High in Vitamins A B2 C, Calcium, Selenium, Zinc, Iron, Potassium. But 46% Sugars. So not too many of them. Cures everything from impotence to malaria according to internet hype. Waitrose do them in the UK. Also called Wolfberries

Ginger: High in Vitamins B1, B2, B5, B6, C, Calcium, Copper, Iron, Magnesium, Manganese, Potassium, Selenium, Zinc, Fibre

Broccoli: High in Vitamins A, B1, B2, B5, B6, B9, C, K, Calcium, Iron, Magnesium, Manganese, Potassium

Carrots: High in Vitamins A, B3, B6, B9, C, K, Manganese, Potassium, Fibre

Tomatoes: High in Vitamins A, B2, B6, B9 C, Potassium, Lycopene

Beetroot: Vitamin B6, B9, C, Iron, Magnesium, Manganese, Phosphorus, Potassium, Zinc, Fibre

Kale: High in Vitamins A, B1, B2, B3, B6, B9, C, K, Calcium, Copper, Iron, Magnesium, Manganese, Potassium

Spinach: High in Vitamins A, B2, B6, B9, C, E, K, Calcium, Copper, Iron. Magnesium, Manganese, Potassium, Fibre

Swiss Chard: High in Vitamins A, C, E, K, Calcium, Copper, Iron, Magensium, Manganese, Potassium, Sodium

Hence we include many Superfood Blast and Smoothie Recipes!

Sleep and Foods

As an example of what food can do for you - here is how diet can help you sleep – without having to take sleeping tablets. If you suffer from insomnia then you may be deficient in an essential amino acid called Tryptophan.

The key players in putting your body to sleep are Serotonin, Melatonin and Tryptophan. All of these can be purchased from health food shops.

The chemical pathway works like this. First the body converts Tryptophan into Tryptophan Hydroxylase (or 5 HydroxyTryptophan or 5HTP). Then this, together with Vitamins. B3, B6, B9 and Magnesium is used to synthesize the neurotransmitter Serotonin. The Serotonin is then converted to the neurohormone Melatonin as necessary

Serotonin is the body's natural sedative. The higher your serotonin levels are the more sleepy you feel. Melatonin controls your body clock, your circadian rhythm, your sleep cycle. These two hormones both put you to sleep and determine how long and how good your sleep quality is.

Tryptophan is one of the essential amino acids – which means that it is essential for human life and the body cannot manufacture it. So we have to eat it!

Just taking 1 gram of Tryptophan can significantly decrease the time it takes to fall asleep and the time you stay asleep for. 6 grams are used to treat certain forms of PMS. 3 grams per day for 2 weeks is prescribed to treat depression and anxiety without the side effects associated with clinical anti depressants like Prosac.So to cheer yourself up eat some foods which are rich in Tryptophan!

Foods which are high in Tryptophan include Chocolate, Eggs, Cheese, Brown rice,

Avocados, Walnuts, Peanuts, Meats, Sesame seeds, Sunflower seeds and Pumpkin seeds. So having a cup of cocoa before you go to bed has a sound basis in biochemistry!

Best Seeds	Tryptophan /100g		Best Greens	Tryptophan /100g
Chia Seeds	721 mg		Parsely	45 mg
Pumpkin Seeds	576 mg		Spinach	39 mg
Sesame Seeds	388 mg		Kale	34 mg
Sunflower Seeds	348 mg		Broccoli	33 mg
Flax Seed	297 mg		Watercress	30 mg
			Swiss Chard	17 mg
			Bok Choy	15 mg

Best Nuts	Tryptophan /100g		Best Veggies	Tryptophan /100g
Cashew Nuts	470 mg		Cauliflower	20 mg
Peanuts	340 mg		Beetroot	19 mg
Walnuts	318 mg		Fine Beans	19 mg
Pistachio Nuts	284 mg		Carrot	12 mg
Almonds	214 mg		Zucchini	10 mg
Hazelnuts	193 mg			
Brazil Nuts	141 mg			
Pecans	93 mg			

Best Fruits	Tryptophan /100g		Foods	Tryptophan /100g
Avocado	26 mg		Cocoa Powder	283 mg
Prunes	25 mg		Dairy Milk	40 mg
Apricots	12 mg		Cheddar Cheese	515 mg
Dates	12 mg		Mozarella Cheese	558 mg
Grapes	11 mg		Egg	210 mg
Oranges	10 mg			
Peaches	10 mg			
Plums	9 mg			
Grapefruits	9 mg			

Some of our Smoothie Recipes are designed to deliver Tryptophan. The RDI is 285 mg. But for a good nights sleep 1000 mg is better. Lots of Chia seeds Cashews Milk Spinach and Prunes and some Cocoa powder will get you to around 475 mg of Tryptophan from one smoothie. That is 166% of the RDI. But you would need 2 of them to really help with sleep that night. Alternatively eat 100 gram of cheese, that would give you another 500 mg of Tryptophan.

Game meat poultry and eggs are also great non blender sources of Tryptophan. If you need something stronger then consider taking the intermediary between Tryptophan and Serotonin - 5HTP as a supplement. Double-blind studies have shown that 5HTP is as effective as Prozac, Paxil, Zoloft, Imipramine and Desipramine and it has less side effects being a natural body compound. 5HTP is cheaper and non prescription being a regular dietary supplement.

Eat a Rainbow of Colour

Red – Lyopene, anthocyanins and other phytonutrients found in red fruits and veggies. Lycopene is a powerful antioxidant that can help reduce the risk of cancer and keep our heart healthy and improve memory function.

White/Tan – Contrary to popular belief, white foods aren't so useless after all! These foods have been shown to reduce the risk of certain cancers, balance hormone levels, lower blood pressure, and boost your body's natural immunity with nutrients such as EGCG and allicin. White fruits and vegetables contain a range of health-promoting phytochemicals such as allicin (found in garlic) which is known for its antiviral and antibacterial properties. Some members of the white group, such as bananas and potatoes, are also a good source of potassium.

Green – Chlorophyll-rich detoxification properties are the most noted value in leafy greens. In addition, luteins, zeaxanthin, along with indoles, help boost greens' cancer-fighting properties, encourage vision health, and help build strong bones and teeth. Green vegetables contain a range of phytochemicals including carotenoids, indoles and saponins, all of which have anti-cancer properties. Leafy greens such as spinach and broccoli are also excellent sources of folate.

Blue/Purple – Phytochemicals anthocyanin and resveratrol promote youthful skin, hair and nails. In addition, these anti-inflammatory compounds may also play a role in cancer-prevention, especially skin cancer and urinary and digestive tract health. They may also reduce the risk of cardio vascular disease.

Orange/Yellow – Foods glowing with orange and yellow are great immune-boosters and vision protectors, mainly due to their high levels of carotenoids. Carotenoids give this group their vibrant colour. A well-known carotenoid called Betacarotene is found in sweet potatoes, pumpkins and carrots. It is converted to vitamin A, which helps maintain healthy mucous membranes and healthy eyes. Another carotenoid called lutein is stored in the eye and has been found to prevent cataracts and age-related macular degeneration, which can lead to blindness.

Nutrition Data

All our Blasts and Smoothies come with full nutritional data giving the precise number of grams of Protein, Carbohydrate, Fat and Fibre for each recipe and the number of Kcals it contains. The data is taken mainly from the USDA database.

Warnings

Do not put your hand or any implement near the blades when the blender is plugged in to an electricity supply.

Cleaning

Use warm water (not hot) and a mild detergent. Rinse the blades and the cups and the base (if necessary) immediately after use to prevent the debris from drying.

Black Flat Leaf Kale not Curly Kale

Kale is a Superfood and is very good for you. But Curly Kale does not taste as good as the other greens in a smoothie in our opinion! To be frank, it tastes like cardboard. However flat leaf Kale (Black Kale or Tuscan Kale or Cavolo Nero), with the leaves pulled off the stems, tastes wonderful and is not too fibrous. So we have specified flat leaf de-stemmed Kale in our recipes.

AVOID THESE INGREDIENTS: Apple Pear Peach Plum Apricot and Cherry **stones and pips** contain cyanide which is very poisonous. These stones and pips *must* therefore be removed before use!

Rhubarb leaves contain oxalate which causes kidney stones, comas, convulsions. 5lb of Rhubarb leaves is fatal!

Tomatoes are fine but the **tomato leaves and vines** are not. They contain alkaloid poisons such as atropine which causes headaches dizziness and vomiting.

Nutmeg: Contains myristicine which is halucingoenic and causes dizziness and vomiting. It is OK in small quantities as a spice but we do not include it in our recipes.

Kidney Beans and **Lima Beans**: These are really really poisonous if eaten raw.

Tips and Extras

Cinnamon and Cloves are lovely in a hot drink but do not really work in a cold one such as a smoothie. We cannot recommend adding sugar given the health difficulties associated with refined sucrose. But the following are fantastic in smoothies...

Ginger Root (sliced up)
Lemon Juice
Lime Juice
Agave Nectar
Honey
Garlic Cloves
Cocoa Powder (a Superfood)
85% Dark Chocolate (a Superfood)
Instant Coffee
Coriander
Parsley
Sage
Chives
Soy Sauce
Whey Protein (Banana, Chocolate, Cookies, Strawberry flavours etc.) – for extra protein
Pea Protein Powder
Soy Protein Powder
Rice Protein Powder

These can be added to any of the recipes for taste.

Superfood Blasts - *Made entirely out of Superfoods*

Broccoli and Chard Rush

Ingredients

1 Cup/Handful of Broccoli Florets (40 grams or 1½ oz)
1 Cup/Handful of Swiss Chard (40 grams or 1½ oz)
¾ Cup of Blackberries (90 grams or 3 oz)
¾ Cup of Avocado slices (90 grams or 3 oz)
22 grams or ¾ oz of Chia Seeds
200 ml / 7 fl oz of Almond Milk (Unsweetened)

Protein 9g, Fat 23g, Carb 10g, Fibre 21g, 336 Kcals

Preparation

Place the nuts or seeds into the Tall Cup. Screw the Nutribullet Extractor Blade on to the top of the cup. Invert the cup, press it down into the Nutribullet Power Base and twist it into place. Blast them for 30 seconds. Put the rest of the solid ingredients into the cup and press them down below the Max Line. Add the fluid base to fill the cup up to the Max Line. Screw the Nutribullet Extractor Blade on to the top of the cup. Invert the cup, press it down into the Nutribullet Power Base and twist it into place. Blast the mixture until it is really smooth (20 or so seconds). *Enjoy!*

Avocado needs Raspberry

Ingredients

2 Cups/Handfuls of Broccoli Florets (80 grams or 3 oz)
¾ Cup of Avocado slices (90 grams or 3 oz)
¾ Cup of Raspberries (90 grams or 3 oz)
22 grams or ¾ oz of Flax Seeds
200 ml / 7 fl oz of Almond Milk (Unsweetened)

Protein 10g, Fat 26g, Carb 10g, Fibre 21g, 361 Kcals

Preparation

Place the nuts or seeds into the Tall Cup. Screw the Nutribullet Extractor Blade on to the top of the cup. Invert the cup, press it down into the Nutribullet Power Base and twist it into place. Blast them for 30 seconds. Put the rest of the solid ingredients into the cup and press them down below the Max Line. Add the fluid base to fill the cup up to the Max Line. Screw the Nutribullet Extractor Blade on to the top of the cup. Invert the cup, press it down into the Nutribullet Power Base and twist it into place. Blast the mixture until it is really smooth (20 or so seconds). *Enjoy!*

Chard on Chia

Ingredients

2 Cups/Handfuls of Swiss Chard (80 grams or 3 oz)
1½ Cups of Blackberries (180 grams or 6 oz)
22 grams or ¾ oz of Chia Seeds
200 ml / 7 fl oz of Almond Milk (Unsweetened)

Protein 8g, Fat 10g, Carb 11g, Fibre 19g, 225 Kcals

Preparation

Place the nuts or seeds into the Tall Cup. Screw the Nutribullet Extractor Blade on to the top of the cup. Invert the cup, press it down into the Nutribullet Power Base and twist it into place. Blast them for 30 seconds. Put the rest of the solid ingredients into the cup and press them down below the Max Line. Add the fluid base to fill the cup up to the Max Line. Screw the Nutribullet Extractor Blade on to the top of the cup. Invert the cup, press it down into the Nutribullet Power Base and twist it into place. Blast the mixture until it is really smooth (20 or so seconds). **Enjoy!**

Broccoli Blossom

Ingredients

1 Cup/Handful of Black Kale de-stemmed (40 grams or 1½ oz)
1 Cup/Handful of Broccoli Florets (40 grams or 1½ oz)
¾ Cup of Papaya (90 grams or 3 oz)
¾ Cup of Avocado slices (90 grams or 3 oz)
22 grams or ¾ oz of Flax Seeds
200 ml / 7 fl oz of Almond Milk (Unsweetened)

Protein 10g, Fat 26g, Carb 13g, Fibre 16g, 353 Kcals

Preparation

Place the nuts or seeds into the Tall Cup. Screw the Nutribullet Extractor Blade on to the top of the cup. Invert the cup, press it down into the Nutribullet Power Base and twist it into place. Blast them for 30 seconds. Put the rest of the solid ingredients into the cup and press them down below the Max Line. Add the fluid base to fill the cup up to the Max Line. Screw the Nutribullet Extractor Blade on to the top of the cup. Invert the cup, press it down into the Nutribullet Power Base and twist it into place. Blast the mixture until it is really smooth (20 or so seconds). **Enjoy!**

Chard Concerto

Ingredients

1 Cup/Handful of Broccoli Florets (40 grams or 1½ oz)
1 Cup/Handful of Swiss Chard (40 grams or 1½ oz)
1½ Cups of Raspberries (180 grams or 6 oz)
22 grams or ¾ oz of Pumpkin Seeds
200 ml / 7 fl oz of Almond Milk (Unsweetened)

Protein 10g, Fat 13g, Carb 15g, Fibre 15g, 265 Kcals

Preparation

Place the nuts or seeds into the Tall Cup. Screw the Nutribullet Extractor Blade on to the top of the cup. Invert the cup, press it down into the Nutribullet Power Base and twist it into place. Blast them for 30 seconds. Put the rest of the solid ingredients into the cup and press them down below the Max Line. Add the fluid base to fill the cup up to the Max Line. Screw the Nutribullet Extractor Blade on to the top of the cup. Invert the cup, press it down into the Nutribullet Power Base and twist it into place. Blast the mixture until it is really smooth (20 or so seconds). **Enjoy!**

Chard and Blackberry Twist

Ingredients

1 Cup/Handful of Black Kale de-stemmed (40 grams or 1½ oz)
1 Cup/Handful of Swiss Chard (40 grams or 1½ oz)
¾ Cup of Guava (90 grams or 3 oz)
¾ Cup of Blackberries (90 grams or 3 oz)
30 grams or 1 oz of Almonds
200 ml / 7 fl oz of Almond Milk (Unsweetened)

Protein 13g, Fat 20g, Carb 16g, Fibre 15g, 324 Kcals

Preparation

Place the nuts or seeds into the Tall Cup. Screw the Nutribullet Extractor Blade on to the top of the cup. Invert the cup, press it down into the Nutribullet Power Base and twist it into place. Blast them for 30 seconds. Put the rest of the solid ingredients into the cup and press them down below the Max Line. Add the fluid base to fill the cup up to the Max Line. Screw the Nutribullet Extractor Blade on to the top of the cup. Invert the cup, press it down into the Nutribullet Power Base and twist it into place. Blast the mixture until it is really smooth (20 or so seconds). **Enjoy!**

Spinach Swirl

Ingredients

1 Cup/Handful of Broccoli Florets (40 grams or 1½ oz)
1 Cup/Handful of Spinach (40 grams or 1½ oz)
1½ Cups of Guava (180 grams or 6 oz)
22 grams or ¾ oz of Flax Seeds
200 ml / 7 fl oz of Almond Milk (Unsweetened)

Protein 12g, Fat 13g, Carb 19g, Fibre 18g, 288 Kcals

Preparation

Place the nuts or seeds into the Tall Cup. Screw the Nutribullet Extractor Blade on to the top of the cup. Invert the cup, press it down into the Nutribullet Power Base and twist it into place. Blast them for 30 seconds. Put the rest of the solid ingredients into the cup and press them down below the Max Line. Add the fluid base to fill the cup up to the Max Line. Screw the Nutribullet Extractor Blade on to the top of the cup. Invert the cup, press it down into the Nutribullet Power Base and twist it into place. Blast the mixture until it is really smooth (20 or so seconds). **Enjoy!**

Black Kale Boost

Ingredients

1 Cup/Handful of Spinach (40 grams or 1½ oz)
1 Cup/Handful of Black Kale de-stemmed (40 grams or 1½ oz)
¾ Cup of Blueberries (90 grams or 3 oz)
¾ Cup of Raspberries (90 grams or 3 oz)
30 grams or 1 oz of Almonds
200 ml / 7 fl oz of Almond Milk (Unsweetened)

Protein 11g, Fat 20g, Carb 19g, Fibre 14g, 324 Kcals

Preparation

Place the nuts or seeds into the Tall Cup. Screw the Nutribullet Extractor Blade on to the top of the cup. Invert the cup, press it down into the Nutribullet Power Base and twist it into place. Blast them for 30 seconds. Put the rest of the solid ingredients into the cup and press them down below the Max Line. Add the fluid base to fill the cup up to the Max Line. Screw the Nutribullet Extractor Blade on to the top of the cup. Invert the cup, press it down into the Nutribullet Power Base and twist it into place. Blast the mixture until it is really smooth (20 or so seconds). **Enjoy!**

Chard and Spinach Tango

Ingredients

1 Cup/Handful of Swiss Chard (40 grams or 1½ oz)
1 Cup/Handful of Spinach (40 grams or 1½ oz)
¾ Cup of Avocado slices (90 grams or 3 oz)
¾ Cup of Raspberries (90 grams or 3 oz)
22 grams or ¾ oz of Pumpkin Seeds
200 ml / 7 fl oz of Dairy Milk Whole

Protein 16g, Fat 31g, Carb 20g, Fibre 15g, 459 Kcals

Preparation

Place the nuts or seeds into the Tall Cup. Screw the Nutribullet Extractor Blade on to the top of the cup. Invert the cup, press it down into the Nutribullet Power Base and twist it into place. Blast them for 30 seconds. Put the rest of the solid ingredients into the cup and press them down below the Max Line. Add the fluid base to fill the cup up to the Max Line. Screw the Nutribullet Extractor Blade on to the top of the cup. Invert the cup, press it down into the Nutribullet Power Base and twist it into place. Blast the mixture until it is really smooth (20 or so seconds). **Enjoy!**

Spinach and Papaya Elixir

Ingredients

1 Cup/Handful of Black Kale de-stemmed (40 grams or 1½ oz)
1 Cup/Handful of Spinach (40 grams or 1½ oz)
1½ Cups of Papaya (180 grams or 6 oz)
30 grams or 1 oz of Almonds
200 ml / 7 fl oz of Almond Milk (Unsweetened)

Protein 11g, Fat 19g, Carb 20g, Fibre 9g, 303 Kcals

Preparation

Place the nuts or seeds into the Tall Cup. Screw the Nutribullet Extractor Blade on to the top of the cup. Invert the cup, press it down into the Nutribullet Power Base and twist it into place. Blast them for 30 seconds. Put the rest of the solid ingredients into the cup and press them down below the Max Line. Add the fluid base to fill the cup up to the Max Line. Screw the Nutribullet Extractor Blade on to the top of the cup. Invert the cup, press it down into the Nutribullet Power Base and twist it into place. Blast the mixture until it is really smooth (20 or so seconds). **Enjoy!**

Superfood Double Fruit Smoothies - *Made entirely out of Superfoods*

Avocado Amazement

Ingredients

1 Cup/Handful of Black Kale de-stemmed (40 grams or 1½ oz)
1 Cup/Handful of Swiss Chard (40 grams or 1½ oz)
1½ Cups of Avocado slices (180 grams or 6 oz)
200 ml / 7 fl oz of Almond Milk (Unsweetened)

Protein 6g, Fat 29g, Carb 5g, Fibre 14g, 335 Kcals

Preparation

Put all the solid ingredients into the Tall Cup and press them down below the Max Line. Add the fluid base to fill the cup up to the Max Line. Screw the Nutribullet Extractor Blade on to the top of the cup. Invert the cup, press it down into the Nutribullet Power Base and twist it into place. Blast the mixture until it is really smooth (20 or so seconds). **Enjoy!**

Broccoli embraces Black Kale

Ingredients

1 Cup/Handful of Broccoli Florets (40 grams or 1½ oz)
1 Cup/Handful of Black Kale de-stemmed (40 grams or 1½ oz)
¾ Cup of Avocado slices (90 grams or 3 oz)
¾ Cup of Raspberries (90 grams or 3 oz)
200 ml / 7 fl oz of Almond Milk (Unsweetened)

Protein 6g, Fat 17g, Carb 9g, Fibre 15g, 244 Kcals

Preparation

Put all the solid ingredients into the Tall Cup and press them down below the Max Line. Add the fluid base to fill the cup up to the Max Line. Screw the Nutribullet Extractor Blade on to the top of the cup. Invert the cup, press it down into the Nutribullet Power Base and twist it into place. Blast the mixture until it is really smooth (20 or so seconds). **Enjoy!**

Chard in Blackberry

Ingredients

1 Cup/Handful of Swiss Chard (40 grams or 1½ oz)
1 Cup/Handful of Spinach (40 grams or 1½ oz)
1½ Cups of Blackberries (180 grams or 6 oz)
200 ml / 7 fl oz of Almond Milk (Unsweetened)

Protein 5g, Fat 3g, Carb 9g, Fibre 12g, 120 Kcals

Preparation

Put all the solid ingredients into the Tall Cup and press them down below the Max Line. Add the fluid base to fill the cup up to the Max Line. Screw the Nutribullet Extractor Blade on to the top of the cup. Invert the cup, press it down into the Nutribullet Power Base and twist it into place. Blast the mixture until it is really smooth (20 or so seconds). **Enjoy!**

Raspberry Royale

Ingredients

1 Cup/Handful of Black Kale de-stemmed (40 grams or 1½ oz)
1 Cup/Handful of Broccoli Florets (40 grams or 1½ oz)
1½ Cups of Raspberries (180 grams or 6 oz)
200 ml / 7 fl oz of Almond Milk (Unsweetened)

Protein 5g, Fat 4g, Carb 12g, Fibre 15g, 147 Kcals

Preparation

Put all the solid ingredients into the Tall Cup and press them down below the Max Line. Add the fluid base to fill the cup up to the Max Line. Screw the Nutribullet Extractor Blade on to the top of the cup. Invert the cup, press it down into the Nutribullet Power Base and twist it into place. Blast the mixture until it is really smooth (20 or so seconds). **Enjoy!**

Broccoli and Avocado Symphony

Ingredients

1 Cup/Handful of Broccoli Florets (40 grams or 1½ oz)
1 Cup/Handful of Black Kale de-stemmed (40 grams or 1½ oz)
¾ Cup of Apricot halves (90 grams or 3 oz)
¾ Cup of Avocado slices (90 grams or 3 oz)
200 ml / 7 fl oz of Almond Milk (Unsweetened)

Protein 6g, Fat 17g, Carb 12g, Fibre 11g, 240 Kcals

Preparation

Put all the solid ingredients into the Tall Cup and press them down below the Max Line. Add the fluid base to fill the cup up to the Max Line. Screw the Nutribullet Extractor Blade on to the top of the cup. Invert the cup, press it down into the Nutribullet Power Base and twist it into place. Blast the mixture until it is really smooth (20 or so seconds). *Enjoy!*

Chard goes Blueberry

Ingredients

1 Cup/Handful of Swiss Chard (40 grams or 1½ oz)
1 Cup/Handful of Spinach (40 grams or 1½ oz)
¾ Cup of Raspberries (90 grams or 3 oz)
¾ Cup of Blueberries (90 grams or 3 oz)
200 ml / 7 fl oz of Almond Milk (Unsweetened)

Protein 4g, Fat 3g, Carb 17g, Fibre 10g, 140 Kcals

Preparation

Put all the solid ingredients into the Tall Cup and press them down below the Max Line. Add the fluid base to fill the cup up to the Max Line. Screw the Nutribullet Extractor Blade on to the top of the cup. Invert the cup, press it down into the Nutribullet Power Base and twist it into place. Blast the mixture until it is really smooth (20 or so seconds). *Enjoy!*

Blueberry Bliss

Ingredients

2 Cups/Handfuls of Swiss Chard (80 grams or 3 oz)
¾ Cup of Raspberries (90 grams or 3 oz)
¾ Cup of Blueberries (90 grams or 3 oz)
200 ml / 7 fl oz of Almond Milk (Unsweetened)

Protein 4g, Fat 3g, Carb 18g, Fibre 10g, 139 Kcals

Preparation

Put all the solid ingredients into the Tall Cup and press them down below the Max Line. Add the fluid base to fill the cup up to the Max Line. Screw the Nutribullet Extractor Blade on to the top of the cup. Invert the cup, press it down into the Nutribullet Power Base and twist it into place. Blast the mixture until it is really smooth (20 or so seconds). **Enjoy!**

Papaya Pizzaz

Ingredients

1 Cup/Handful of Black Kale de-stemmed (40 grams or 1½ oz)
1 Cup/Handful of Spinach (40 grams or 1½ oz)
¾ Cup of Guava (90 grams or 3 oz)
¾ Cup of Papaya (90 grams or 3 oz)
200 ml / 7 fl oz of Almond Milk (Unsweetened)

Protein 6g, Fat 4g, Carb 18g, Fibre 9g, 149 Kcals

Preparation

Put all the solid ingredients into the Tall Cup and press them down below the Max Line. Add the fluid base to fill the cup up to the Max Line. Screw the Nutribullet Extractor Blade on to the top of the cup. Invert the cup, press it down into the Nutribullet Power Base and twist it into place. Blast the mixture until it is really smooth (20 or so seconds). **Enjoy!**

Guava Galaxy

Ingredients

2 Cups/Handfuls of Black Kale de-stemmed (80 grams or 3 oz)
¾ Cup of Guava (90 grams or 3 oz)
¾ Cup of Apricot halves (90 grams or 3 oz)
200 ml / 7 fl oz of Almond Milk (Unsweetened)

Protein 7g, Fat 5g, Carb 18g, Fibre 9g, 158 Kcals

Preparation

Put all the solid ingredients into the Tall Cup and press them down below the Max Line. Add the fluid base to fill the cup up to the Max Line. Screw the Nutribullet Extractor Blade on to the top of the cup. Invert the cup, press it down into the Nutribullet Power Base and twist it into place. Blast the mixture until it is really smooth (20 or so seconds). **Enjoy!**

Broccoli loves Papaya

Ingredients

2 Cups/Handfuls of Broccoli Florets (80 grams or 3 oz)
¾ Cup of Papaya (90 grams or 3 oz)
¾ Cup of Apricot halves (90 grams or 3 oz)
200 ml / 7 fl oz of Almond Milk (Unsweetened)

Protein 5g, Fat 3g, Carb 20g, Fibre 6g, 135 Kcals

Preparation

Put all the solid ingredients into the Tall Cup and press them down below the Max Line. Add the fluid base to fill the cup up to the Max Line. Screw the Nutribullet Extractor Blade on to the top of the cup. Invert the cup, press it down into the Nutribullet Power Base and twist it into place. Blast the mixture until it is really smooth (20 or so seconds). **Enjoy!**

Superfood Fruit and Veggie Blasts - *Made entirely out of Superfoods*

Blackberry and Flax Regatta

Ingredients

1 Cup/Handful of Black Kale de-stemmed (40 grams or 1½ oz)
1 Cup/Handful of Broccoli Florets (40 grams or 1½ oz)
¾ Cup of Blackberries (90 grams or 3 oz)
1 Cup/Handful of sliced Asparagus (120 grams or 4 oz)
22 grams or ¾ oz of Flax Seeds
200 ml / 7 fl oz of Almond Milk (Unsweetened)

Protein 11g, Fat 13g, Carb 9g, Fibre 16g, 233 Kcals

Preparation

Place the nuts or seeds into the Tall Cup. Screw the Nutribullet Extractor Blade on to the top of the cup. Invert the cup, press it down into the Nutribullet Power Base and twist it into place. Blast them for 30 seconds. Put the rest of the solid ingredients into the cup and press them down below the Max Line. Add the fluid base to fill the cup up to the Max Line. Screw the Nutribullet Extractor Blade on to the top of the cup. Invert the cup, press it down into the Nutribullet Power Base and twist it into place. Blast the mixture until it is really smooth (20 or so seconds). ***Enjoy!***

Tomato Therapy

Ingredients

2 Cups/Handfuls of Black Kale de-stemmed (80 grams or 3 oz)
¾ Cup of Blackberries (90 grams or 3 oz)
1 Cup/Handful of sliced Tomato (120 grams or 4 oz)
22 grams or ¾ oz of Flax Seeds
200 ml / 7 fl oz of Almond Milk (Unsweetened)

Protein 10g, Fat 13g, Carb 9g, Fibre 15g, 231 Kcals

Preparation

Place the nuts or seeds into the Tall Cup. Screw the Nutribullet Extractor Blade on to the top of the cup. Invert the cup, press it down into the Nutribullet Power Base and twist it into place. Blast them for 30 seconds. Put the rest of the solid ingredients into the cup and press them down below the Max Line. Add the fluid base to fill the cup up to the Max Line. Screw the Nutribullet Extractor Blade on to the top of the cup. Invert the cup, press it down into the Nutribullet Power Base and twist it into place. Blast the mixture until it is really smooth (20 or so seconds). ***Enjoy!***

Black Kale and Broccoli Seduction

Ingredients

1 Cup/Handful of Black Kale de-stemmed (40 grams or 1½ oz)
1 Cup/Handful of Broccoli Florets (40 grams or 1½ oz)
¾ Cup of Raspberries (90 grams or 3 oz)
1 Cup/Handful of sliced Asparagus (120 grams or 4 oz)
22 grams or ¾ oz of Pumpkin Seeds
200 ml / 7 fl oz of Almond Milk (Unsweetened)

Protein 12g, Fat 13g, Carb 12g, Fibre 12g, 248 Kcals

Preparation

Place the nuts or seeds into the Tall Cup. Screw the Nutribullet Extractor Blade on to the top of the cup. Invert the cup, press it down into the Nutribullet Power Base and twist it into place. Blast them for 30 seconds. Put the rest of the solid ingredients into the cup and press them down below the Max Line. Add the fluid base to fill the cup up to the Max Line. Screw the Nutribullet Extractor Blade on to the top of the cup. Invert the cup, press it down into the Nutribullet Power Base and twist it into place. Blast the mixture until it is really smooth (20 or so seconds). **Enjoy!**

Flax Forever

Ingredients

2 Cups/Handfuls of Swiss Chard (80 grams or 3 oz)
¾ Cup of Apricot halves (90 grams or 3 oz)
1 Cup/Handful of sliced Asparagus (120 grams or 4 oz)
22 grams or ¾ oz of Flax Seeds
200 ml / 7 fl oz of Almond Milk (Unsweetened)

Protein 10g, Fat 12g, Carb 13g, Fibre 12g, 225 Kcals

Preparation

Place the nuts or seeds into the Tall Cup. Screw the Nutribullet Extractor Blade on to the top of the cup. Invert the cup, press it down into the Nutribullet Power Base and twist it into place. Blast them for 30 seconds. Put the rest of the solid ingredients into the cup and press them down below the Max Line. Add the fluid base to fill the cup up to the Max Line. Screw the Nutribullet Extractor Blade on to the top of the cup. Invert the cup, press it down into the Nutribullet Power Base and twist it into place. Blast the mixture until it is really smooth (20 or so seconds). **Enjoy!**

Guava and Asparagus Creation

Ingredients

1 Cup/Handful of Broccoli Florets (40 grams or 1½ oz)
1 Cup/Handful of Black Kale de-stemmed (40 grams or 1½ oz)
¾ Cup of Guava (90 grams or 3 oz)
1 Cup/Handful of sliced Asparagus (120 grams or 4 oz)
30 grams or 1 oz of Almonds
200 ml / 7 fl oz of Almond Milk (Unsweetened)

Protein 15g, Fat 20g, Carb 15g, Fibre 13g, 315 Kcals

Preparation

Place the nuts or seeds into the Tall Cup. Screw the Nutribullet Extractor Blade on to the top of the cup. Invert the cup, press it down into the Nutribullet Power Base and twist it into place. Blast them for 30 seconds. Put the rest of the solid ingredients into the cup and press them down below the Max Line. Add the fluid base to fill the cup up to the Max Line. Screw the Nutribullet Extractor Blade on to the top of the cup. Invert the cup, press it down into the Nutribullet Power Base and twist it into place. Blast the mixture until it is really smooth (20 or so seconds). **Enjoy!**

Papaya joins Chia

Ingredients

1 Cup/Handful of Broccoli Florets (40 grams or 1½ oz)
1 Cup/Handful of Black Kale de-stemmed (40 grams or 1½ oz)
¾ Cup of Papaya (90 grams or 3 oz)
1 Cup/Handful of sliced Tomato (120 grams or 4 oz)
22 grams or ¾ oz of Chia Seeds
200 ml / 7 fl oz of Almond Milk (Unsweetened)

Protein 8g, Fat 10g, Carb 16g, Fibre 13g, 220 Kcals

Preparation

Place the nuts or seeds into the Tall Cup. Screw the Nutribullet Extractor Blade on to the top of the cup. Invert the cup, press it down into the Nutribullet Power Base and twist it into place. Blast them for 30 seconds. Put the rest of the solid ingredients into the cup and press them down below the Max Line. Add the fluid base to fill the cup up to the Max Line. Screw the Nutribullet Extractor Blade on to the top of the cup. Invert the cup, press it down into the Nutribullet Power Base and twist it into place. Blast the mixture until it is really smooth (20 or so seconds). **Enjoy!**

Asparagus Adventure

Ingredients

2 Cups/Handfuls of Spinach (80 grams or 3 oz)
¾ Cup of Avocado slices (90 grams or 3 oz)
1 Cup/Handful of sliced Asparagus (120 grams or 4 oz)
22 grams or ¾ oz of Chia Seeds
200 ml / 7 fl oz of Dairy Milk Whole

Protein 17g, Fat 28g, Carb 16g, Fibre 18g, 421 Kcals

Preparation

Place the nuts or seeds into the Tall Cup. Screw the Nutribullet Extractor Blade on to the top of the cup. Invert the cup, press it down into the Nutribullet Power Base and twist it into place. Blast them for 30 seconds. Put the rest of the solid ingredients into the cup and press them down below the Max Line. Add the fluid base to fill the cup up to the Max Line. Screw the Nutribullet Extractor Blade on to the top of the cup. Invert the cup, press it down into the Nutribullet Power Base and twist it into place. Blast the mixture until it is really smooth (20 or so seconds). *Enjoy!*

Spinach meets Avocado

Ingredients

1 Cup/Handful of Spinach (40 grams or 1½ oz)
1 Cup/Handful of Black Kale de-stemmed (40 grams or 1½ oz)
¾ Cup of Avocado slices (90 grams or 3 oz)
1 Cup/Handful of sliced Asparagus (120 grams or 4 oz)
22 grams or ¾ oz of Chia Seeds
200 ml / 7 fl oz of Dairy Milk Whole

Protein 17g, Fat 28g, Carb 16g, Fibre 18g, 426 Kcals

Preparation

Place the nuts or seeds into the Tall Cup. Screw the Nutribullet Extractor Blade on to the top of the cup. Invert the cup, press it down into the Nutribullet Power Base and twist it into place. Blast them for 30 seconds. Put the rest of the solid ingredients into the cup and press them down below the Max Line. Add the fluid base to fill the cup up to the Max Line. Screw the Nutribullet Extractor Blade on to the top of the cup. Invert the cup, press it down into the Nutribullet Power Base and twist it into place. Blast the mixture until it is really smooth (20 or so seconds). *Enjoy!*

Almond Anthem

Ingredients

2 Cups/Handfuls of Broccoli Florets (80 grams or 3 oz)
¾ Cup of Guava (90 grams or 3 oz)
1 Cup/Handful of sliced Tomato (120 grams or 4 oz)
30 grams or 1 oz of Almonds
200 ml / 7 fl oz of Almond Milk (Unsweetened)

Protein 13g, Fat 19g, Carb 17g, Fibre 12g, 313 Kcals

Preparation

Place the nuts or seeds into the Tall Cup. Screw the Nutribullet Extractor Blade on to the top of the cup. Invert the cup, press it down into the Nutribullet Power Base and twist it into place. Blast them for 30 seconds. Put the rest of the solid ingredients into the cup and press them down below the Max Line. Add the fluid base to fill the cup up to the Max Line. Screw the Nutribullet Extractor Blade on to the top of the cup. Invert the cup, press it down into the Nutribullet Power Base and twist it into place. Blast the mixture until it is really smooth (20 or so seconds). **Enjoy!**

Carrot Cornucopia

Ingredients

1 Cup/Handful of Black Kale de-stemmed (40 grams or 1½ oz)
1 Cup/Handful of Spinach (40 grams or 1½ oz)
¾ Cup of Papaya (90 grams or 3 oz)
1 Cup/Handful of sliced Carrots (120 grams or 4 oz)
22 grams or ¾ oz of Flax Seeds
200 ml / 7 fl oz of Almond Milk (Unsweetened)

Protein 9g, Fat 13g, Carb 18g, Fibre 14g, 254 Kcals

Preparation

Place the nuts or seeds into the Tall Cup. Screw the Nutribullet Extractor Blade on to the top of the cup. Invert the cup, press it down into the Nutribullet Power Base and twist it into place. Blast them for 30 seconds. Put the rest of the solid ingredients into the cup and press them down below the Max Line. Add the fluid base to fill the cup up to the Max Line. Screw the Nutribullet Extractor Blade on to the top of the cup. Invert the cup, press it down into the Nutribullet Power Base and twist it into place. Blast the mixture until it is really smooth (20 or so seconds). **Enjoy!**

Superfood Fruit and Veggie Smoothies - *Made entirely out of Superfoods*

Avocado and Asparagus Piazza

Ingredients

1 Cup/Handful of Swiss Chard (40 grams or 1½ oz)
1 Cup/Handful of Broccoli Florets (40 grams or 1½ oz)
¾ Cup of Avocado slices (90 grams or 3 oz)
1 Cup/Handful of sliced Asparagus (120 grams or 4 oz)
200 ml / 7 fl oz of Almond Milk (Unsweetened)

Protein 7g, Fat 16g, Carb 7g, Fibre 11g, 215 Kcals

Preparation

Put all the solid ingredients into the Tall Cup and press them down below the Max Line. Add the fluid base to fill the cup up to the Max Line. Screw the Nutribullet Extractor Blade on to the top of the cup. Invert the cup, press it down into the Nutribullet Power Base and twist it into place. Blast the mixture until it is really smooth (20 or so seconds). *Enjoy!*

Papaya embraces Tomato

Ingredients

1 Cup/Handful of Black Kale de-stemmed (40 grams or 1½ oz)
1 Cup/Handful of Spinach (40 grams or 1½ oz)
¾ Cup of Papaya (90 grams or 3 oz)
1 Cup/Handful of sliced Tomato (120 grams or 4 oz)
200 ml / 7 fl oz of Almond Milk (Unsweetened)

Protein 5g, Fat 3g, Carb 13g, Fibre 6g, 109 Kcals

Preparation

Put all the solid ingredients into the Tall Cup and press them down below the Max Line. Add the fluid base to fill the cup up to the Max Line. Screw the Nutribullet Extractor Blade on to the top of the cup. Invert the cup, press it down into the Nutribullet Power Base and twist it into place. Blast the mixture until it is really smooth (20 or so seconds). *Enjoy!*

Guava on Asparagus

Ingredients

1 Cup/Handful of Swiss Chard (40 grams or 1½ oz)
1 Cup/Handful of Broccoli Florets (40 grams or 1½ oz)
¾ Cup of Guava (90 grams or 3 oz)
1 Cup/Handful of sliced Asparagus (120 grams or 4 oz)
200 ml / 7 fl oz of Almond Milk (Unsweetened)

Protein 8g, Fat 3g, Carb 13g, Fibre 10g, 132 Kcals

Preparation

Put all the solid ingredients into the Tall Cup and press them down below the Max Line. Add the fluid base to fill the cup up to the Max Line. Screw the Nutribullet Extractor Blade on to the top of the cup. Invert the cup, press it down into the Nutribullet Power Base and twist it into place. Blast the mixture until it is really smooth (20 or so seconds). **Enjoy!**

Papaya needs Asparagus

Ingredients

1 Cup/Handful of Broccoli Florets (40 grams or 1½ oz)
1 Cup/Handful of Black Kale de-stemmed (40 grams or 1½ oz)
¾ Cup of Papaya (90 grams or 3 oz)
1 Cup/Handful of sliced Asparagus (120 grams or 4 oz)
200 ml / 7 fl oz of Almond Milk (Unsweetened)

Protein 6g, Fat 3g, Carb 13g, Fibre 7g, 116 Kcals

Preparation

Put all the solid ingredients into the Tall Cup and press them down below the Max Line. Add the fluid base to fill the cup up to the Max Line. Screw the Nutribullet Extractor Blade on to the top of the cup. Invert the cup, press it down into the Nutribullet Power Base and twist it into place. Blast the mixture until it is really smooth (20 or so seconds). **Enjoy!**

Papaya and Tomato Extracted

Ingredients

1 Cup/Handful of Swiss Chard (40 grams or 1½ oz)
1 Cup/Handful of Spinach (40 grams or 1½ oz)
¾ Cup of Papaya (90 grams or 3 oz)
1 Cup/Handful of sliced Tomato (120 grams or 4 oz)
200 ml / 7 fl oz of Almond Milk (Unsweetened)

Protein 4g, Fat 3g, Carb 13g, Fibre 5g, 103 Kcals

Preparation

Put all the solid ingredients into the Tall Cup and press them down below the Max Line. Add the fluid base to fill the cup up to the Max Line. Screw the Nutribullet Extractor Blade on to the top of the cup. Invert the cup, press it down into the Nutribullet Power Base and twist it into place. Blast the mixture until it is really smooth (20 or so seconds). **Enjoy!**

Apricot Avarice

Ingredients

1 Cup/Handful of Swiss Chard (40 grams or 1½ oz)
1 Cup/Handful of Broccoli Florets (40 grams or 1½ oz)
¾ Cup of Apricot halves (90 grams or 3 oz)
1 Cup/Handful of sliced Asparagus (120 grams or 4 oz)
200 ml / 7 fl oz of Almond Milk (Unsweetened)

Protein 7g, Fat 3g, Carb 13g, Fibre 7g, 114 Kcals

Preparation

Put all the solid ingredients into the Tall Cup and press them down below the Max Line. Add the fluid base to fill the cup up to the Max Line. Screw the Nutribullet Extractor Blade on to the top of the cup. Invert the cup, press it down into the Nutribullet Power Base and twist it into place. Blast the mixture until it is really smooth (20 or so seconds). **Enjoy!**

Raspberry and Beetroot Lagoon

Ingredients

1 Cup/Handful of Swiss Chard (40 grams or 1½ oz)
1 Cup/Handful of Spinach (40 grams or 1½ oz)
¾ Cup of Raspberries (90 grams or 3 oz)
1 Cup/Handful of diced Beetroot (120 grams or 4 oz)
200 ml / 7 fl oz of Almond Milk (Unsweetened)

Protein 6g, Fat 3g, Carb 15g, Fibre 12g, 141 Kcals

Preparation

Put all the solid ingredients into the Tall Cup and press them down below the Max Line. Add the fluid base to fill the cup up to the Max Line. Screw the Nutribullet Extractor Blade on to the top of the cup. Invert the cup, press it down into the Nutribullet Power Base and twist it into place. Blast the mixture until it is really smooth (20 or so seconds). **Enjoy!**

Avocado loves Asparagus

Ingredients

2 Cups/Handfuls of Swiss Chard (80 grams or 3 oz)
¾ Cup of Avocado slices (90 grams or 3 oz)
1 Cup/Handful of sliced Asparagus (120 grams or 4 oz)
200 ml / 7 fl oz of Dairy Milk Whole

Protein 12g, Fat 21g, Carb 15g, Fibre 10g, 311 Kcals

Preparation

Put all the solid ingredients into the Tall Cup and press them down below the Max Line. Add the fluid base to fill the cup up to the Max Line. Screw the Nutribullet Extractor Blade on to the top of the cup. Invert the cup, press it down into the Nutribullet Power Base and twist it into place. Blast the mixture until it is really smooth (20 or so seconds). **Enjoy!**

Raspberry meets Carrot

Ingredients

1 Cup/Handful of Swiss Chard (40 grams or 1½ oz)
1 Cup/Handful of Broccoli Florets (40 grams or 1½ oz)
¾ Cup of Raspberries (90 grams or 3 oz)
1 Cup/Handful of sliced Carrots (120 grams or 4 oz)
200 ml / 7 fl oz of Almond Milk (Unsweetened)

Protein 5g, Fat 3g, Carb 16g, Fibre 12g, 143 Kcals

Preparation

Put all the solid ingredients into the Tall Cup and press them down below the Max Line. Add the fluid base to fill the cup up to the Max Line. Screw the Nutribullet Extractor Blade on to the top of the cup. Invert the cup, press it down into the Nutribullet Power Base and twist it into place. Blast the mixture until it is really smooth (20 or so seconds). *Enjoy!*

Beetroot Blizzard

Ingredients

2 Cups/Handfuls of Black Kale de-stemmed (80 grams or 3 oz)
¾ Cup of Apricot halves (90 grams or 3 oz)
1 Cup/Handful of diced Beetroot (120 grams or 4 oz)
200 ml / 7 fl oz of Almond Milk (Unsweetened)

Protein 7g, Fat 4g, Carb 18g, Fibre 8g, 148 Kcals

Preparation

Put all the solid ingredients into the Tall Cup and press them down below the Max Line. Add the fluid base to fill the cup up to the Max Line. Screw the Nutribullet Extractor Blade on to the top of the cup. Invert the cup, press it down into the Nutribullet Power Base and twist it into place. Blast the mixture until it is really smooth (20 or so seconds). *Enjoy!*

Heart Care Double Fruit Blasts
Anti-inflammatory, high in Omega 3, anti oxidants, Vitamins C, E

Blackberry and Walnut Waistline

Ingredients

1 Cup/Handful of Spinach (40 grams or 1½ oz)
1 Cup/Handful of Lettuce Leaves (40 grams or 1½ oz)
1½ Cups of Blackberries (180 grams or 6 oz)
30 grams or 1 oz of Walnuts
200 ml / 7 fl oz of Almond Milk (Unsweetened)

Protein 10g, Fat 23g, Carb 11g, Fibre 14g, 315 Kcals

Preparation

Place the nuts or seeds into the Tall Cup. Screw the Nutribullet Extractor Blade on to the top of the cup. Invert the cup, press it down into the Nutribullet Power Base and twist it into place. Blast them for 30 seconds. Put the rest of the solid ingredients into the cup and press them down below the Max Line. Add the fluid base to fill the cup up to the Max Line. Screw the Nutribullet Extractor Blade on to the top of the cup. Invert the cup, press it down into the Nutribullet Power Base and twist it into place. Blast the mixture until it is really smooth (20 or so seconds). ***Enjoy!***

Lettuce goes Pecan

Ingredients

1 Cup/Handful of Lettuce Leaves (40 grams or 1½ oz)
1 Cup/Handful of Rocket/Arugura Lettuce (40 grams or 1½ oz)
¾ Cup of Strawberries (90 grams or 3 oz)
¾ Cup of Blackberries (90 grams or 3 oz)
30 grams or 1 oz of Pecans
200 ml / 7 fl oz of Almond Milk (Unsweetened)

Protein 6g, Fat 25g, Carb 12g, Fibre 12g, 313 Kcals

Preparation

Place the nuts or seeds into the Tall Cup. Screw the Nutribullet Extractor Blade on to the top of the cup. Invert the cup, press it down into the Nutribullet Power Base and twist it into place. Blast them for 30 seconds. Put the rest of the solid ingredients into the cup and press them down below the Max Line. Add the fluid base to fill the cup up to the Max Line. Screw the Nutribullet Extractor Blade on to the top of the cup. Invert the cup, press it down into the Nutribullet Power Base and twist it into place. Blast the mixture until it is really smooth (20 or so seconds). ***Enjoy!***

Orange and Pecan Healer

Ingredients

1 Cup/Handful of Spinach (40 grams or 1½ oz)
1 Cup/Handful of Black Kale de-stemmed (40 grams or 1½ oz)
¾ Cup of Orange segments (90 grams or 3 oz)
¾ Cup of Blackberries (90 grams or 3 oz)
30 grams or 1 oz of Pecans
200 ml / 7 fl oz of Almond Milk (Unsweetened)

Protein 8g, Fat 25g, Carb 15g, Fibre 12g, 337 Kcals

Preparation

Place the nuts or seeds into the Tall Cup. Screw the Nutribullet Extractor Blade on to the top of the cup. Invert the cup, press it down into the Nutribullet Power Base and twist it into place. Blast them for 30 seconds. Put the rest of the solid ingredients into the cup and press them down below the Max Line. Add the fluid base to fill the cup up to the Max Line. Screw the Nutribullet Extractor Blade on to the top of the cup. Invert the cup, press it down into the Nutribullet Power Base and twist it into place. Blast the mixture until it is really smooth (20 or so seconds). **Enjoy!**

Raspberry and Orange Anthem

Ingredients

1 Cup/Handful of Broccoli Florets (40 grams or 1½ oz)
1 Cup/Handful of Spinach (40 grams or 1½ oz)
¾ Cup of Raspberries (90 grams or 3 oz)
¾ Cup of Orange segments (90 grams or 3 oz)
22 grams or ¾ oz of Sesame Seeds Hulled
200 ml / 7 fl oz of Almond Milk (Unsweetened)

Protein 9g, Fat 16g, Carb 16g, Fibre 12g, 269 Kcals

Preparation

Place the nuts or seeds into the Tall Cup. Screw the Nutribullet Extractor Blade on to the top of the cup. Invert the cup, press it down into the Nutribullet Power Base and twist it into place. Blast them for 30 seconds. Put the rest of the solid ingredients into the cup and press them down below the Max Line. Add the fluid base to fill the cup up to the Max Line. Screw the Nutribullet Extractor Blade on to the top of the cup. Invert the cup, press it down into the Nutribullet Power Base and twist it into place. Blast the mixture until it is really smooth (20 or so seconds). **Enjoy!**

Orange Orchestra

Ingredients

1 Cup/Handful of Rocket/Arugura Lettuce (40 grams or 1½ oz)
1 Cup/Handful of Broccoli Florets (40 grams or 1½ oz)
¾ Cup of Orange segments (90 grams or 3 oz)
¾ Cup of Raspberries (90 grams or 3 oz)
22 grams or ¾ oz of Sesame Seeds Hulled
200 ml / 7 fl oz of Almond Milk (Unsweetened)

Protein 8g, Fat 16g, Carb 16g, Fibre 12g, 266 Kcals

Preparation

Place the nuts or seeds into the Tall Cup. Screw the Nutribullet Extractor Blade on to the top of the cup. Invert the cup, press it down into the Nutribullet Power Base and twist it into place. Blast them for 30 seconds. Put the rest of the solid ingredients into the cup and press them down below the Max Line. Add the fluid base to fill the cup up to the Max Line. Screw the Nutribullet Extractor Blade on to the top of the cup. Invert the cup, press it down into the Nutribullet Power Base and twist it into place. Blast the mixture until it is really smooth (20 or so seconds). *Enjoy!*

Chia City

Ingredients

1 Cup/Handful of Lettuce Leaves (40 grams or 1½ oz)
1 Cup/Handful of Spinach (40 grams or 1½ oz)
¾ Cup of Clementine slices (90 grams or 3 oz)
¾ Cup of Blackberries (90 grams or 3 oz)
22 grams or ¾ oz of Chia Seeds
200 ml / 7 fl oz of Almond Milk (Unsweetened)

Protein 8g, Fat 10g, Carb 16g, Fibre 16g, 229 Kcals

Preparation

Place the nuts or seeds into the Tall Cup. Screw the Nutribullet Extractor Blade on to the top of the cup. Invert the cup, press it down into the Nutribullet Power Base and twist it into place. Blast them for 30 seconds. Put the rest of the solid ingredients into the cup and press them down below the Max Line. Add the fluid base to fill the cup up to the Max Line. Screw the Nutribullet Extractor Blade on to the top of the cup. Invert the cup, press it down into the Nutribullet Power Base and twist it into place. Blast the mixture until it is really smooth (20 or so seconds). *Enjoy!*

Black Kale and Rocket Invigorator

Ingredients

1 Cup/Handful of Black Kale de-stemmed (40 grams or 1½ oz)
1 Cup/Handful of Rocket/Arugura Lettuce (40 grams or 1½ oz)
¾ Cup of Tangerine slices (90 grams or 3 oz)
¾ Cup of Raspberries (90 grams or 3 oz)
22 grams or ¾ oz of Flax Seeds
200 ml / 7 fl oz of Almond Milk (Unsweetened)

Protein 9g, Fat 13g, Carb 17g, Fibre 16g, 257 Kcals

Preparation

Place the nuts or seeds into the Tall Cup. Screw the Nutribullet Extractor Blade on to the top of the cup. Invert the cup, press it down into the Nutribullet Power Base and twist it into place. Blast them for 30 seconds. Put the rest of the solid ingredients into the cup and press them down below the Max Line. Add the fluid base to fill the cup up to the Max Line. Screw the Nutribullet Extractor Blade on to the top of the cup. Invert the cup, press it down into the Nutribullet Power Base and twist it into place. Blast the mixture until it is really smooth (20 or so seconds). **Enjoy!**

Spinach and Clementine Reaction

Ingredients

1 Cup/Handful of Broccoli Florets (40 grams or 1½ oz)
1 Cup/Handful of Spinach (40 grams or 1½ oz)
¾ Cup of Clementine slices (90 grams or 3 oz)
¾ Cup of Strawberries (90 grams or 3 oz)
30 grams or 1 oz of Walnuts
200 ml / 7 fl oz of Almond Milk (Unsweetened)

Protein 9g, Fat 22g, Carb 19g, Fibre 8g, 316 Kcals

Preparation

Place the nuts or seeds into the Tall Cup. Screw the Nutribullet Extractor Blade on to the top of the cup. Invert the cup, press it down into the Nutribullet Power Base and twist it into place. Blast them for 30 seconds. Put the rest of the solid ingredients into the cup and press them down below the Max Line. Add the fluid base to fill the cup up to the Max Line. Screw the Nutribullet Extractor Blade on to the top of the cup. Invert the cup, press it down into the Nutribullet Power Base and twist it into place. Blast the mixture until it is really smooth (20 or so seconds). **Enjoy!**

Blackberry Breeze

Ingredients

2 Cups/Handfuls of Black Kale de-stemmed (80 grams or 3 oz)
¾ Cup of Blackberries (90 grams or 3 oz)
¾ Cup of Pomegranate seeds (90 grams or 3 oz)
22 grams or ¾ oz of Flax Seeds
200 ml / 7 fl oz of Almond Milk (Unsweetened)

Protein 10g, Fat 14g, Carb 19g, Fibre 17g, 284 Kcals

Preparation

Place the nuts or seeds into the Tall Cup. Screw the Nutribullet Extractor Blade on to the top of the cup. Invert the cup, press it down into the Nutribullet Power Base and twist it into place. Blast them for 30 seconds. Put the rest of the solid ingredients into the cup and press them down below the Max Line. Add the fluid base to fill the cup up to the Max Line. Screw the Nutribullet Extractor Blade on to the top of the cup. Invert the cup, press it down into the Nutribullet Power Base and twist it into place. Blast the mixture until it is really smooth (20 or so seconds). **Enjoy!**

Nectarine and Guava Scene

Ingredients

2 Cups/Handfuls of Broccoli Florets (80 grams or 3 oz)
¾ Cup of Nectarine segments (90 grams or 3 oz)
¾ Cup of Guava (90 grams or 3 oz)
22 grams or ¾ oz of Sesame Seeds Hulled
200 ml / 7 fl oz of Almond Milk (Unsweetened)

Protein 10g, Fat 16g, Carb 20g, Fibre 11g, 285 Kcals

Preparation

Place the nuts or seeds into the Tall Cup. Screw the Nutribullet Extractor Blade on to the top of the cup. Invert the cup, press it down into the Nutribullet Power Base and twist it into place. Blast them for 30 seconds. Put the rest of the solid ingredients into the cup and press them down below the Max Line. Add the fluid base to fill the cup up to the Max Line. Screw the Nutribullet Extractor Blade on to the top of the cup. Invert the cup, press it down into the Nutribullet Power Base and twist it into place. Blast the mixture until it is really smooth (20 or so seconds). **Enjoy!**

Heart Care Fruit & Veggie Blasts
Anti-inflammatory, high in Omega 3, anti oxidants, Vitamins C, E

Lettuce Lagoon

Ingredients

1 Cup/Handful of Lettuce Leaves (40 grams or 1½ oz)
1 Cup/Handful of Spinach (40 grams or 1½ oz)
¾ Cup of Blackberries (90 grams or 3 oz)
1 Cup/Handful of sliced Tomato (120 grams or 4 oz)
22 grams or ¾ oz of Flax Seeds
200 ml / 7 fl oz of Almond Milk (Unsweetened)
Protein 9g, Fat 12g, Carb 9g, Fibre 15g, 219 Kcals

Preparation

Place the nuts or seeds into the Tall Cup. Screw the Nutribullet Extractor Blade on to the top of the cup. Invert the cup, press it down into the Nutribullet Power Base and twist it into place. Blast them for 30 seconds. Put the rest of the solid ingredients into the cup and press them down below the Max Line. Add the fluid base to fill the cup up to the Max Line. Screw the Nutribullet Extractor Blade on to the top of the cup. Invert the cup, press it down into the Nutribullet Power Base and twist it into place. Blast the mixture until it is really smooth (20 or so seconds). **Enjoy!**

Red Pepper Recovery

Ingredients

1 Cup/Handful of Spinach (40 grams or 1½ oz)
1 Cup/Handful of Lettuce Leaves (40 grams or 1½ oz)
¾ Cup of Strawberries (90 grams or 3 oz)
1 Cup/Handful of sliced Red Pepper (120 grams or 4 oz)
22 grams or ¾ oz of Sesame Seeds Hulled
200 ml / 7 fl oz of Almond Milk (Unsweetened)
Protein 8g, Fat 16g, Carb 11g, Fibre 9g, 239 Kcals

Preparation

Place the nuts or seeds into the Tall Cup. Screw the Nutribullet Extractor Blade on to the top of the cup. Invert the cup, press it down into the Nutribullet Power Base and twist it into place. Blast them for 30 seconds. Put the rest of the solid ingredients into the cup and press them down below the Max Line. Add the fluid base to fill the cup up to the Max Line. Screw the Nutribullet Extractor Blade on to the top of the cup. Invert the cup, press it down into the Nutribullet Power Base and twist it into place. Blast the mixture until it is really smooth (20 or so seconds). **Enjoy!**

Blackberry in Tomato

Ingredients

2 Cups/Handfuls of Broccoli Florets (80 grams or 3 oz)
¾ Cup of Blackberries (90 grams or 3 oz)
1 Cup/Handful of sliced Tomato (120 grams or 4 oz)
30 grams or 1 oz of Pecans
200 ml / 7 fl oz of Almond Milk (Unsweetened)

Protein 8g, Fat 25g, Carb 12g, Fibre 12g, 320 Kcals

Preparation

Place the nuts or seeds into the Tall Cup. Screw the Nutribullet Extractor Blade on to the top of the cup. Invert the cup, press it down into the Nutribullet Power Base and twist it into place. Blast them for 30 seconds. Put the rest of the solid ingredients into the cup and press them down below the Max Line. Add the fluid base to fill the cup up to the Max Line. Screw the Nutribullet Extractor Blade on to the top of the cup. Invert the cup, press it down into the Nutribullet Power Base and twist it into place. Blast the mixture until it is really smooth (20 or so seconds). **Enjoy!**

Pecan Panacea

Ingredients

1 Cup/Handful of Lettuce Leaves (40 grams or 1½ oz)
1 Cup/Handful of Spinach (40 grams or 1½ oz)
¾ Cup of Guava (90 grams or 3 oz)
1 Cup/Handful of sliced Asparagus (120 grams or 4 oz)
30 grams or 1 oz of Pecans
200 ml / 7 fl oz of Almond Milk (Unsweetened)

Protein 10g, Fat 25g, Carb 13g, Fibre 13g, 334 Kcals

Preparation

Place the nuts or seeds into the Tall Cup. Screw the Nutribullet Extractor Blade on to the top of the cup. Invert the cup, press it down into the Nutribullet Power Base and twist it into place. Blast them for 30 seconds. Put the rest of the solid ingredients into the cup and press them down below the Max Line. Add the fluid base to fill the cup up to the Max Line. Screw the Nutribullet Extractor Blade on to the top of the cup. Invert the cup, press it down into the Nutribullet Power Base and twist it into place. Blast the mixture until it is really smooth (20 or so seconds). **Enjoy!**

Cauliflower Constellation

Ingredients

1 Cup/Handful of Rocket/Arugura Lettuce (40 grams or 1½ oz)
1 Cup/Handful of Spinach (40 grams or 1½ oz)
¾ Cup of Nectarine segments (90 grams or 3 oz)
1 Cup/Handful of sliced Cauliflower florets (120 grams or 4 oz)
22 grams or ¾ oz of Flax Seeds
200 ml / 7 fl oz of Almond Milk (Unsweetened)

Protein 10g, Fat 12g, Carb 13g, Fibre 12g, 228 Kcals

Preparation

Place the nuts or seeds into the Tall Cup. Screw the Nutribullet Extractor Blade on to the top of the cup. Invert the cup, press it down into the Nutribullet Power Base and twist it into place. Blast them for 30 seconds. Put the rest of the solid ingredients into the cup and press them down below the Max Line. Add the fluid base to fill the cup up to the Max Line. Screw the Nutribullet Extractor Blade on to the top of the cup. Invert the cup, press it down into the Nutribullet Power Base and twist it into place. Blast the mixture until it is really smooth (20 or so seconds). **Enjoy!**

Lettuce joins Walnut

Ingredients

2 Cups/Handfuls of Lettuce Leaves (80 grams or 3 oz)
¾ Cup of Orange segments (90 grams or 3 oz)
1 Cup/Handful of sliced Tomato (120 grams or 4 oz)
30 grams or 1 oz of Walnuts
200 ml / 7 fl oz of Almond Milk (Unsweetened)

Protein 8g, Fat 22g, Carb 15g, Fibre 8g, 299 Kcals

Preparation

Place the nuts or seeds into the Tall Cup. Screw the Nutribullet Extractor Blade on to the top of the cup. Invert the cup, press it down into the Nutribullet Power Base and twist it into place. Blast them for 30 seconds. Put the rest of the solid ingredients into the cup and press them down below the Max Line. Add the fluid base to fill the cup up to the Max Line. Screw the Nutribullet Extractor Blade on to the top of the cup. Invert the cup, press it down into the Nutribullet Power Base and twist it into place. Blast the mixture until it is really smooth (20 or so seconds). **Enjoy!**

Rocket Reaction

Ingredients

1 Cup/Handful of Spinach (40 grams or 1½ oz)
1 Cup/Handful of Rocket/Arugura Lettuce (40 grams or 1½ oz)
¾ Cup of Clementine slices (90 grams or 3 oz)
1 Cup/Handful of sliced Asparagus (120 grams or 4 oz)
30 grams or 1 oz of Walnuts
200 ml / 7 fl oz of Almond Milk (Unsweetened)

Protein 10g, Fat 22g, Carb 15g, Fibre 8g, 303 Kcals

Preparation

Place the nuts or seeds into the Tall Cup. Screw the Nutribullet Extractor Blade on to the top of the cup. Invert the cup, press it down into the Nutribullet Power Base and twist it into place. Blast them for 30 seconds. Put the rest of the solid ingredients into the cup and press them down below the Max Line. Add the fluid base to fill the cup up to the Max Line. Screw the Nutribullet Extractor Blade on to the top of the cup. Invert the cup, press it down into the Nutribullet Power Base and twist it into place. Blast the mixture until it is really smooth (20 or so seconds). *Enjoy!*

Blueberry loves Pecan

Ingredients

1 Cup/Handful of Black Kale de-stemmed (40 grams or 1½ oz)
1 Cup/Handful of Broccoli Florets (40 grams or 1½ oz)
¾ Cup of Blueberries (90 grams or 3 oz)
1 Cup/Handful of sliced Tomato (120 grams or 4 oz)
30 grams or 1 oz of Pecans
200 ml / 7 fl oz of Almond Milk (Unsweetened)

Protein 8g, Fat 25g, Carb 18g, Fibre 9g, 333 Kcals

Preparation

Place the nuts or seeds into the Tall Cup. Screw the Nutribullet Extractor Blade on to the top of the cup. Invert the cup, press it down into the Nutribullet Power Base and twist it into place. Blast them for 30 seconds. Put the rest of the solid ingredients into the cup and press them down below the Max Line. Add the fluid base to fill the cup up to the Max Line. Screw the Nutribullet Extractor Blade on to the top of the cup. Invert the cup, press it down into the Nutribullet Power Base and twist it into place. Blast the mixture until it is really smooth (20 or so seconds). *Enjoy!*

Sesame Salad

Ingredients

1 Cup/Handful of Rocket/Arugura Lettuce (40 grams or 1½ oz)
1 Cup/Handful of Broccoli Florets (40 grams or 1½ oz)
¾ Cup of Nectarine segments (90 grams or 3 oz)
1 Cup/Handful of sliced Carrots (120 grams or 4 oz)
22 grams or ¾ oz of Sesame Seeds Hulled
200 ml / 7 fl oz of Almond Milk (Unsweetened)

Protein 9g, Fat 16g, Carb 19g, Fibre 9g, 265 Kcals

Preparation

Place the nuts or seeds into the Tall Cup. Screw the Nutribullet Extractor Blade on to the top of the cup. Invert the cup, press it down into the Nutribullet Power Base and twist it into place. Blast them for 30 seconds. Put the rest of the solid ingredients into the cup and press them down below the Max Line. Add the fluid base to fill the cup up to the Max Line. Screw the Nutribullet Extractor Blade on to the top of the cup. Invert the cup, press it down into the Nutribullet Power Base and twist it into place. Blast the mixture until it is really smooth (20 or so seconds). **Enjoy!**

Guava and Chia Detente

Ingredients

1 Cup/Handful of Spinach (40 grams or 1½ oz)
1 Cup/Handful of Lettuce Leaves (40 grams or 1½ oz)
¾ Cup of Guava (90 grams or 3 oz)
1 Cup/Handful of sliced Carrots (120 grams or 4 oz)
22 grams or ¾ oz of Chia Seeds
200 ml / 7 fl oz of Almond Milk (Unsweetened)

Protein 10g, Fat 10g, Carb 19g, Fibre 18g, 259 Kcals

Preparation

Place the nuts or seeds into the Tall Cup. Screw the Nutribullet Extractor Blade on to the top of the cup. Invert the cup, press it down into the Nutribullet Power Base and twist it into place. Blast them for 30 seconds. Put the rest of the solid ingredients into the cup and press them down below the Max Line. Add the fluid base to fill the cup up to the Max Line. Screw the Nutribullet Extractor Blade on to the top of the cup. Invert the cup, press it down into the Nutribullet Power Base and twist it into place. Blast the mixture until it is really smooth (20 or so seconds). **Enjoy!**

Happiness, Deep Sleep and Stress Busting Blasts
High in Tryptophan, Magnesium,. Vits B3, B6, B9

Peanut Paradise

Ingredients

1 Cup/Handful of Watercress (40 grams or 1½ oz)
1 Cup/Handful of Spinach (40 grams or 1½ oz)
¾ Cup of Avocado slices (90 grams or 3 oz)
1 Cup/Handful of sliced Cauliflower florets (120 grams or 4 oz)
30 grams or 1 oz of Peanuts
200 ml / 7 fl oz of Almond Milk (Unsweetened)
Protein 15g, Fat 31g, Carb 9g, Fibre 13g, 383 Kcals

Preparation

Place the nuts or seeds into the Tall Cup. Screw the Nutribullet Extractor Blade on to the top of the cup. Invert the cup, press it down into the Nutribullet Power Base and twist it into place. Blast them for 30 seconds. Put the rest of the solid ingredients into the cup and press them down below the Max Line. Add the fluid base to fill the cup up to the Max Line. Screw the Nutribullet Extractor Blade on to the top of the cup. Invert the cup, press it down into the Nutribullet Power Base and twist it into place. Blast the mixture until it is really smooth (20 or so seconds). *Enjoy!*

Fine Bean Feast

Ingredients

1 Cup/Handful of Broccoli Florets (40 grams or 1½ oz)
1 Cup/Handful of Spinach (40 grams or 1½ oz)
¾ Cup of Avocado slices (90 grams or 3 oz)
1 Cup/Handful of sliced Fine Beans (120 grams or 4 oz)
22 grams or ¾ oz of Sunflower Seeds Hulled
200 ml / 7 fl oz of Almond Milk (Unsweetened)
Protein 12g, Fat 27g, Carb 11g, Fibre 13g, 336 Kcals

Preparation

Place the nuts or seeds into the Tall Cup. Screw the Nutribullet Extractor Blade on to the top of the cup. Invert the cup, press it down into the Nutribullet Power Base and twist it into place. Blast them for 30 seconds. Put the rest of the solid ingredients into the cup and press them down below the Max Line. Add the fluid base to fill the cup up to the Max Line. Screw the Nutribullet Extractor Blade on to the top of the cup. Invert the cup, press it down into the Nutribullet Power Base and twist it into place. Blast the mixture until it is really smooth (20 or so seconds). *Enjoy!*

Avocado joins Carrot

Ingredients

2 Cups/Handfuls of Broccoli Florets (80 grams or 3 oz)
¾ Cup of Avocado slices (90 grams or 3 oz)
1 Cup/Handful of sliced Carrots (120 grams or 4 oz)
22 grams or ¾ oz of Sesame Seeds Hulled
200 ml / 7 fl oz of Almond Milk (Unsweetened)

Protein 10g, Fat 29g, Carb 13g, Fibre 14g, 377 Kcals

Preparation

Place the nuts or seeds into the Tall Cup. Screw the Nutribullet Extractor Blade on to the top of the cup. Invert the cup, press it down into the Nutribullet Power Base and twist it into place. Blast them for 30 seconds. Put the rest of the solid ingredients into the cup and press them down below the Max Line. Add the fluid base to fill the cup up to the Max Line. Screw the Nutribullet Extractor Blade on to the top of the cup. Invert the cup, press it down into the Nutribullet Power Base and twist it into place. Blast the mixture until it is really smooth (20 or so seconds). **Enjoy!**

Watercress Waistline

Ingredients

1 Cup/Handful of Broccoli Florets (40 grams or 1½ oz)
1 Cup/Handful of Watercress (40 grams or 1½ oz)
¾ Cup of Avocado slices (90 grams or 3 oz)
1 Cup/Handful of diced Beetroot (120 grams or 4 oz)
30 grams or 1 oz of Peanuts
200 ml / 7 fl oz of Almond Milk (Unsweetened)

Protein 14g, Fat 31g, Carb 14g, Fibre 14g, 409 Kcals

Preparation

Place the nuts or seeds into the Tall Cup. Screw the Nutribullet Extractor Blade on to the top of the cup. Invert the cup, press it down into the Nutribullet Power Base and twist it into place. Blast them for 30 seconds. Put the rest of the solid ingredients into the cup and press them down below the Max Line. Add the fluid base to fill the cup up to the Max Line. Screw the Nutribullet Extractor Blade on to the top of the cup. Invert the cup, press it down into the Nutribullet Power Base and twist it into place. Blast the mixture until it is really smooth (20 or so seconds). **Enjoy!**

Pumpkin Potion

Ingredients

1 Cup/Handful of Broccoli Florets (40 grams or 1½ oz)
1 Cup/Handful of Spinach (40 grams or 1½ oz)
¾ Cup of Avocado slices (90 grams or 3 oz)
1 Cup/Handful of sliced Carrots (120 grams or 4 oz)
22 grams or ¾ oz of Pumpkin Seeds
200 ml / 7 fl oz of Almond Milk (Unsweetened)

Protein 11g, Fat 26g, Carb 14g, Fibre 13g, 366 Kcals

Preparation

Place the nuts or seeds into the Tall Cup. Screw the Nutribullet Extractor Blade on to the top of the cup. Invert the cup, press it down into the Nutribullet Power Base and twist it into place. Blast them for 30 seconds. Put the rest of the solid ingredients into the cup and press them down below the Max Line. Add the fluid base to fill the cup up to the Max Line. Screw the Nutribullet Extractor Blade on to the top of the cup. Invert the cup, press it down into the Nutribullet Power Base and twist it into place. Blast the mixture until it is really smooth (20 or so seconds). ***Enjoy!***

Spinach and Apricot Fantasy

Ingredients

1 Cup/Handful of Watercress (40 grams or 1½ oz)
1 Cup/Handful of Spinach (40 grams or 1½ oz)
¾ Cup of Apricot halves (90 grams or 3 oz)
1 Cup/Handful of sliced Cauliflower florets (120 grams or 4 oz)
30 grams or 1 oz of Walnuts
200 ml / 7 fl oz of Almond Milk (Unsweetened)

Protein 11g, Fat 23g, Carb 15g, Fibre 8g, 308 Kcals

Preparation

Place the nuts or seeds into the Tall Cup. Screw the Nutribullet Extractor Blade on to the top of the cup. Invert the cup, press it down into the Nutribullet Power Base and twist it into place. Blast them for 30 seconds. Put the rest of the solid ingredients into the cup and press them down below the Max Line. Add the fluid base to fill the cup up to the Max Line. Screw the Nutribullet Extractor Blade on to the top of the cup. Invert the cup, press it down into the Nutribullet Power Base and twist it into place. Blast the mixture until it is really smooth (20 or so seconds). ***Enjoy!***

Watercress meets Sesame

Ingredients

1 Cup/Handful of Spinach (40 grams or 1½ oz)
1 Cup/Handful of Watercress (40 grams or 1½ oz)
¾ Cup of Apricot halves (90 grams or 3 oz)
1 Cup/Handful of sliced Carrots (120 grams or 4 oz)
22 grams or ¾ oz of Sesame Seeds Hulled
200 ml / 7 fl oz of Almond Milk (Unsweetened)

Protein 9g, Fat 16g, Carb 18g, Fibre 9g, 263 Kcals

Preparation

Place the nuts or seeds into the Tall Cup. Screw the Nutribullet Extractor Blade on to the top of the cup. Invert the cup, press it down into the Nutribullet Power Base and twist it into place. Blast them for 30 seconds. Put the rest of the solid ingredients into the cup and press them down below the Max Line. Add the fluid base to fill the cup up to the Max Line. Screw the Nutribullet Extractor Blade on to the top of the cup. Invert the cup, press it down into the Nutribullet Power Base and twist it into place. Blast the mixture until it is really smooth (20 or so seconds). **Enjoy!**

Watercress and Sunflower Consortium

Ingredients

2 Cups/Handfuls of Watercress (80 grams or 3 oz)
¾ Cup of Avocado slices (90 grams or 3 oz)
1 Cup/Handful of sliced Fine Beans (120 grams or 4 oz)
22 grams or ¾ oz of Sunflower Seeds Hulled
200 ml / 7 fl oz of Dairy Milk Semi Skimmed

Protein 17g, Fat 28g, Carb 18g, Fibre 10g, 396 Kcals

Preparation

Place the nuts or seeds into the Tall Cup. Screw the Nutribullet Extractor Blade on to the top of the cup. Invert the cup, press it down into the Nutribullet Power Base and twist it into place. Blast them for 30 seconds. Put the rest of the solid ingredients into the cup and press them down below the Max Line. Add the fluid base to fill the cup up to the Max Line. Screw the Nutribullet Extractor Blade on to the top of the cup. Invert the cup, press it down into the Nutribullet Power Base and twist it into place. Blast the mixture until it is really smooth (20 or so seconds). **Enjoy!**

Spinach embraces Chia

Ingredients

1 Cup/Handful of Watercress (40 grams or 1½ oz)
1 Cup/Handful of Spinach (40 grams or 1½ oz)
¾ Cup of Apricot halves (90 grams or 3 oz)
1 Cup/Handful of diced Beetroot (120 grams or 4 oz)
22 grams or ¾ oz of Chia Seeds
200 ml / 7 fl oz of Almond Milk (Unsweetened)

Protein 10g, Fat 10g, Carb 19g, Fibre 15g, 241 Kcals

Preparation

Place the nuts or seeds into the Tall Cup. Screw the Nutribullet Extractor Blade on to the top of the cup. Invert the cup, press it down into the Nutribullet Power Base and twist it into place. Blast them for 30 seconds. Put the rest of the solid ingredients into the cup and press them down below the Max Line. Add the fluid base to fill the cup up to the Max Line. Screw the Nutribullet Extractor Blade on to the top of the cup. Invert the cup, press it down into the Nutribullet Power Base and twist it into place. Blast the mixture until it is really smooth (20 or so seconds). **Enjoy!**

Broccoli goes Avocado

Ingredients

1 Cup/Handful of Broccoli Florets (40 grams or 1½ oz)
1 Cup/Handful of Watercress (40 grams or 1½ oz)
¾ Cup of Avocado slices (90 grams or 3 oz)
1 Cup/Handful of sliced Fine Beans (120 grams or 4 oz)
22 grams or ¾ oz of Pumpkin Seeds
200 ml / 7 fl oz of Dairy Milk Semi Skimmed

Protein 19g, Fat 27g, Carb 19g, Fibre 11g, 416 Kcals

Preparation

Place the nuts or seeds into the Tall Cup. Screw the Nutribullet Extractor Blade on to the top of the cup. Invert the cup, press it down into the Nutribullet Power Base and twist it into place. Blast them for 30 seconds. Put the rest of the solid ingredients into the cup and press them down below the Max Line. Add the fluid base to fill the cup up to the Max Line. Screw the Nutribullet Extractor Blade on to the top of the cup. Invert the cup, press it down into the Nutribullet Power Base and twist it into place. Blast the mixture until it is really smooth (20 or so seconds). **Enjoy!**

Detoxing and Cleansing Smoothies
All ingredients have detoxing capabilities

Verdant Amazement

Ingredients

2 Cups/Handfuls of Watercress (80 grams or 3 oz)
¾ Cup of Avocado slices (90 grams or 3 oz)
1 Cup/Handful of sliced Asparagus (120 grams or 4 oz)
200 ml / 7 fl oz of Almond Milk (Unsweetened)

Protein 7g, Fat 16g, Carb 5g, Fibre 10g, 202 Kcals

Preparation

Put all the solid ingredients into the Tall Cup and press them down below the Max Line. Add the fluid base to fill the cup up to the Max Line. Screw the Nutribullet Extractor Blade on to the top of the cup. Invert the cup, press it down into the Nutribullet Power Base and twist it into place. Blast the mixture until it is really smooth (20 or so seconds). **Enjoy!**

Red Cabbage on Black Kale

Ingredients

1 Cup/Handful of Red or White Cabbage (40 grams or 1½ oz)
1 Cup/Handful of Black Kale de-stemmed (40 grams or 1½ oz)
¾ Cup of Avocado slices (90 grams or 3 oz)
1 Cup/Handful of sliced Asparagus (120 grams or 4 oz)
200 ml / 7 fl oz of Almond Milk (Unsweetened)

Protein 7g, Fat 16g, Carb 7g, Fibre 11g, 220 Kcals

Preparation

Put all the solid ingredients into the Tall Cup and press them down below the Max Line. Add the fluid base to fill the cup up to the Max Line. Screw the Nutribullet Extractor Blade on to the top of the cup. Invert the cup, press it down into the Nutribullet Power Base and twist it into place. Blast the mixture until it is really smooth (20 or so seconds). **Enjoy!**

Grapefruit Guru

Ingredients

2 Cups/Handfuls of Black Kale de-stemmed (80 grams or 3 oz)
¾ Cup of Grapefruit segments (90 grams or 3 oz)
1 Cup/Handful of sliced Asparagus (120 grams or 4 oz)
200 ml / 7 fl oz of Almond Milk (Unsweetened)

Protein 7g, Fat 4g, Carb 10g, Fibre 6g, 106 Kcals

Preparation

Put all the solid ingredients into the Tall Cup and press them down below the Max Line. Add the fluid base to fill the cup up to the Max Line. Screw the Nutribullet Extractor Blade on to the top of the cup. Invert the cup, press it down into the Nutribullet Power Base and twist it into place. Blast the mixture until it is really smooth (20 or so seconds). **Enjoy!**

Green Cabbage Gala

Ingredients

1 Cup/Handful of Broccoli Florets (40 grams or 1½ oz)
1 Cup/Handful of Green Cabbage (40 grams or 1½ oz)
¾ Cup of Grapefruit segments (90 grams or 3 oz)
1 Cup/Handful of sliced Asparagus (120 grams or 4 oz)
200 ml / 7 fl oz of Almond Milk (Unsweetened)

Protein 6g, Fat 3g, Carb 12g, Fibre 6g, 102 Kcals

Preparation

Put all the solid ingredients into the Tall Cup and press them down below the Max Line. Add the fluid base to fill the cup up to the Max Line. Screw the Nutribullet Extractor Blade on to the top of the cup. Invert the cup, press it down into the Nutribullet Power Base and twist it into place. Blast the mixture until it is really smooth (20 or so seconds). **Enjoy!**

Watercress needs Avocado

Ingredients

1 Cup/Handful of Watercress (40 grams or 1½ oz)
1 Cup/Handful of Red or White Cabbage (40 grams or 1½ oz)
¾ Cup of Avocado slices (90 grams or 3 oz)
1 Cup/Handful of diced Beetroot (120 grams or 4 oz)
200 ml / 7 fl oz of Almond Milk (Unsweetened)

Protein 6g, Fat 16g, Carb 12g, Fibre 11g, 238 Kcals

Preparation

Put all the solid ingredients into the Tall Cup and press them down below the Max Line. Add the fluid base to fill the cup up to the Max Line. Screw the Nutribullet Extractor Blade on to the top of the cup. Invert the cup, press it down into the Nutribullet Power Base and twist it into place. Blast the mixture until it is really smooth (20 or so seconds). **Enjoy!**

Fennel Fusion

Ingredients

1 Cup/Handful of Fennel (40 grams or 1½ oz)
1 Cup/Handful of Green Cabbage (40 grams or 1½ oz)
¾ Cup of Avocado slices (90 grams or 3 oz)
1 Cup/Handful of diced Beetroot (120 grams or 4 oz)
200 ml / 7 fl oz of Almond Milk (Unsweetened)

Protein 6g, Fat 16g, Carb 13g, Fibre 12g, 244 Kcals

Preparation

Put all the solid ingredients into the Tall Cup and press them down below the Max Line. Add the fluid base to fill the cup up to the Max Line. Screw the Nutribullet Extractor Blade on to the top of the cup. Invert the cup, press it down into the Nutribullet Power Base and twist it into place. Blast the mixture until it is really smooth (20 or so seconds). **Enjoy!**

Black Kale and Apple Mirage

Ingredients

1 Cup/Handful of Black Kale de-stemmed (40 grams or 1½ oz)
1 Cup/Handful of Watercress (40 grams or 1½ oz)
¾ Cup of Apple slices (90 grams or 3 oz)
1 Cup/Handful of sliced Asparagus (120 grams or 4 oz)
200 ml / 7 fl oz of Almond Milk (Unsweetened)

Protein 6g, Fat 3g, Carb 14g, Fibre 7g, 115 Kcals

Preparation

Put all the solid ingredients into the Tall Cup and press them down below the Max Line. Add the fluid base to fill the cup up to the Max Line. Screw the Nutribullet Extractor Blade on to the top of the cup. Invert the cup, press it down into the Nutribullet Power Base and twist it into place. Blast the mixture until it is really smooth (20 or so seconds). **Enjoy!**

Pineapple Panache

Ingredients

1 Cup/Handful of Watercress (40 grams or 1½ oz)
1 Cup/Handful of Broccoli Florets (40 grams or 1½ oz)
¾ Cup of Pineapple chunks (90 grams or 3 oz)
1 Cup/Handful of sliced Asparagus (120 grams or 4 oz)
200 ml / 7 fl oz of Almond Milk (Unsweetened)

Protein 6g, Fat 3g, Carb 15g, Fibre 6g, 113 Kcals

Preparation

Put all the solid ingredients into the Tall Cup and press them down below the Max Line. Add the fluid base to fill the cup up to the Max Line. Screw the Nutribullet Extractor Blade on to the top of the cup. Invert the cup, press it down into the Nutribullet Power Base and twist it into place. Blast the mixture until it is really smooth (20 or so seconds). **Enjoy!**

Broccoli in Pineapple

Ingredients

1 Cup/Handful of Fennel (40 grams or 1½ oz)
1 Cup/Handful of Broccoli Florets (40 grams or 1½ oz)
¾ Cup of Pineapple chunks (90 grams or 3 oz)
1 Cup/Handful of sliced Asparagus (120 grams or 4 oz)
200 ml / 7 fl oz of Almond Milk (Unsweetened)

Protein 6g, Fat 3g, Carb 16g, Fibre 7g, 121 Kcals

Preparation

Put all the solid ingredients into the Tall Cup and press them down below the Max Line. Add the fluid base to fill the cup up to the Max Line. Screw the Nutribullet Extractor Blade on to the top of the cup. Invert the cup, press it down into the Nutribullet Power Base and twist it into place. Blast the mixture until it is really smooth (20 or so seconds). **Enjoy!**

Grapefruit and Beetroot Galaxy

Ingredients

2 Cups/Handfuls of Broccoli Florets (80 grams or 3 oz)
¾ Cup of Grapefruit segments (90 grams or 3 oz)
1 Cup/Handful of diced Beetroot (120 grams or 4 oz)
200 ml / 7 fl oz of Almond Milk (Unsweetened)

Protein 6g, Fat 3g, Carb 18g, Fibre 7g, 133 Kcals

Preparation

Put all the solid ingredients into the Tall Cup and press them down below the Max Line. Add the fluid base to fill the cup up to the Max Line. Screw the Nutribullet Extractor Blade on to the top of the cup. Invert the cup, press it down into the Nutribullet Power Base and twist it into place. Blast the mixture until it is really smooth (20 or so seconds). **Enjoy!**

Clear Thinking Brain Food Blasts - *High in Omega3, Beta Carotene, Lycopene, Magnesium, Zinc, Vitamins B, C, E*

Avocado and Brazil Energizer

Ingredients

1 Cup/Handful of Mint (40 grams or 1½ oz)
1 Cup/Handful of Watercress (40 grams or 1½ oz)
¾ Cup of Avocado slices (90 grams or 3 oz)
1 Cup/Handful of sliced Carrots (120 grams or 4 oz)
30 grams or 1 oz of Brazil nuts
200 ml / 7 fl oz of Almond Milk (Unsweetened)

Protein 10g, Fat 36g, Carb 12g, Fibre 15g, 438 Kcals

Preparation

Place the nuts or seeds into the Tall Cup. Screw the Nutribullet Extractor Blade on to the top of the cup. Invert the cup, press it down into the Nutribullet Power Base and twist it into place. Blast them for 30 seconds. Put the rest of the solid ingredients into the cup and press them down below the Max Line. Add the fluid base to fill the cup up to the Max Line. Screw the Nutribullet Extractor Blade on to the top of the cup. Invert the cup, press it down into the Nutribullet Power Base and twist it into place. Blast the mixture until it is really smooth (20 or so seconds). **Enjoy!**

Spinach meets Flax

Ingredients

2 Cups/Handfuls of Spinach (80 grams or 3 oz)
¾ Cup of Blackberries (90 grams or 3 oz)
1 Cup/Handful of sliced Tomato (120 grams or 4 oz)
22 grams or ¾ oz of Flax Seeds
200 ml / 7 fl oz of Coconut Milk

Protein 9g, Fat 12g, Carb 14g, Fibre 14g, 236 Kcals

Preparation

Place the nuts or seeds into the Tall Cup. Screw the Nutribullet Extractor Blade on to the top of the cup. Invert the cup, press it down into the Nutribullet Power Base and twist it into place. Blast them for 30 seconds. Put the rest of the solid ingredients into the cup and press them down below the Max Line. Add the fluid base to fill the cup up to the Max Line. Screw the Nutribullet Extractor Blade on to the top of the cup. Invert the cup, press it down into the Nutribullet Power Base and twist it into place. Blast the mixture until it is really smooth (20 or so seconds). **Enjoy!**

Bok Choy Blend

Ingredients

1 Cup/Handful of Bok Choy (40 grams or 1½ oz)
1 Cup/Handful of Rocket/Arugura Lettuce (40 grams or 1½ oz)
¾ Cup of Avocado slices (90 grams or 3 oz)
1 Cup/Handful of sliced Tomato (120 grams or 4 oz)
30 grams or 1 oz of Almonds
200 ml / 7 fl oz of Hazelnut Milk

Protein 11g, Fat 33g, Carb 14g, Fibre 12g, 411 Kcals

Preparation

Place the nuts or seeds into the Tall Cup. Screw the Nutribullet Extractor Blade on to the top of the cup. Invert the cup, press it down into the Nutribullet Power Base and twist it into place. Blast them for 30 seconds. Put the rest of the solid ingredients into the cup and press them down below the Max Line. Add the fluid base to fill the cup up to the Max Line. Screw the Nutribullet Extractor Blade on to the top of the cup. Invert the cup, press it down into the Nutribullet Power Base and twist it into place. Blast the mixture until it is really smooth (20 or so seconds). *Enjoy!*

Green Cabbage joins Sesame

Ingredients

2 Cups/Handfuls of Green Cabbage (80 grams or 3 oz)
¾ Cup of Blackberries (90 grams or 3 oz)
1 Cup/Handful of sliced Tomato (120 grams or 4 oz)
22 grams or ¾ oz of Sesame Seeds Hulled
200 ml / 7 fl oz of Coconut Milk

Protein 8g, Fat 15g, Carb 15g, Fibre 10g, 251 Kcals

Preparation

Place the nuts or seeds into the Tall Cup. Screw the Nutribullet Extractor Blade on to the top of the cup. Invert the cup, press it down into the Nutribullet Power Base and twist it into place. Blast them for 30 seconds. Put the rest of the solid ingredients into the cup and press them down below the Max Line. Add the fluid base to fill the cup up to the Max Line. Screw the Nutribullet Extractor Blade on to the top of the cup. Invert the cup, press it down into the Nutribullet Power Base and twist it into place. Blast the mixture until it is really smooth (20 or so seconds). *Enjoy!*

Watercress and Rocket Nexus

Ingredients

1 Cup/Handful of Watercress (40 grams or 1½ oz)
1 Cup/Handful of Rocket/Arugura Lettuce (40 grams or 1½ oz)
¾ Cup of Blackberries (90 grams or 3 oz)
1 Cup/Handful of sliced Tomato (120 grams or 4 oz)
30 grams or 1 oz of Walnuts
200 ml / 7 fl oz of Hazelnut Milk

Protein 9g, Fat 24g, Carb 16g, Fibre 10g, 324 Kcals

Preparation

Place the nuts or seeds into the Tall Cup. Screw the Nutribullet Extractor Blade on to the top of the cup. Invert the cup, press it down into the Nutribullet Power Base and twist it into place. Blast them for 30 seconds. Put the rest of the solid ingredients into the cup and press them down below the Max Line. Add the fluid base to fill the cup up to the Max Line. Screw the Nutribullet Extractor Blade on to the top of the cup. Invert the cup, press it down into the Nutribullet Power Base and twist it into place. Blast the mixture until it is really smooth (20 or so seconds). **Enjoy!**

Blackberry and Carrot Vortex

Ingredients

1 Cup/Handful of Rocket/Arugura Lettuce (40 grams or 1½ oz)
1 Cup/Handful of Green Cabbage (40 grams or 1½ oz)
¾ Cup of Blackberries (90 grams or 3 oz)
1 Cup/Handful of sliced Carrots (120 grams or 4 oz)
22 grams or ¾ oz of Pumpkin Seeds
200 ml / 7 fl oz of Almond Milk (Unsweetened)

Protein 10g, Fat 13g, Carb 16g, Fibre 12g, 254 Kcals

Preparation

Place the nuts or seeds into the Tall Cup. Screw the Nutribullet Extractor Blade on to the top of the cup. Invert the cup, press it down into the Nutribullet Power Base and twist it into place. Blast them for 30 seconds. Put the rest of the solid ingredients into the cup and press them down below the Max Line. Add the fluid base to fill the cup up to the Max Line. Screw the Nutribullet Extractor Blade on to the top of the cup. Invert the cup, press it down into the Nutribullet Power Base and twist it into place. Blast the mixture until it is really smooth (20 or so seconds). **Enjoy!**

Rocket in Blueberry

Ingredients

1 Cup/Handful of Mint (40 grams or 1½ oz)
1 Cup/Handful of Rocket/Arugura Lettuce (40 grams or 1½ oz)
¾ Cup of Blueberries (90 grams or 3 oz)
1 Cup/Handful of sliced Tomato (120 grams or 4 oz)
30 grams or 1 oz of Hazelnuts
200 ml / 7 fl oz of Almond Milk (Unsweetened)

Protein 9g, Fat 21g, Carb 18g, Fibre 11g, 310 Kcals

Preparation

Place the nuts or seeds into the Tall Cup. Screw the Nutribullet Extractor Blade on to the top of the cup. Invert the cup, press it down into the Nutribullet Power Base and twist it into place. Blast them for 30 seconds. Put the rest of the solid ingredients into the cup and press them down below the Max Line. Add the fluid base to fill the cup up to the Max Line. Screw the Nutribullet Extractor Blade on to the top of the cup. Invert the cup, press it down into the Nutribullet Power Base and twist it into place. Blast the mixture until it is really smooth (20 or so seconds). **Enjoy!**

Mint Miracle

Ingredients

1 Cup/Handful of Spinach (40 grams or 1½ oz)
1 Cup/Handful of Mint (40 grams or 1½ oz)
¾ Cup of Avocado slices (90 grams or 3 oz)
1 Cup/Handful of sliced Carrots (120 grams or 4 oz)
30 grams or 1 oz of Pecans
200 ml / 7 fl oz of Hazelnut Milk

Protein 9g, Fat 39g, Carb 18g, Fibre 16g, 485 Kcals

Preparation

Place the nuts or seeds into the Tall Cup. Screw the Nutribullet Extractor Blade on to the top of the cup. Invert the cup, press it down into the Nutribullet Power Base and twist it into place. Blast them for 30 seconds. Put the rest of the solid ingredients into the cup and press them down below the Max Line. Add the fluid base to fill the cup up to the Max Line. Screw the Nutribullet Extractor Blade on to the top of the cup. Invert the cup, press it down into the Nutribullet Power Base and twist it into place. Blast the mixture until it is really smooth (20 or so seconds). **Enjoy!**

Bok Choy loves Rocket

Ingredients

1 Cup/Handful of Bok Choy (40 grams or 1½ oz)
1 Cup/Handful of Rocket/Arugura Lettuce (40 grams or 1½ oz)
¾ Cup of Avocado slices (90 grams or 3 oz)
1 Cup/Handful of sliced Carrots (120 grams or 4 oz)
30 grams or 1 oz of Almonds
200 ml / 7 fl oz of Coconut Milk

Protein 11g, Fat 31g, Carb 18g, Fibre 13g, 421 Kcals

Preparation

Place the nuts or seeds into the Tall Cup. Screw the Nutribullet Extractor Blade on to the top of the cup. Invert the cup, press it down into the Nutribullet Power Base and twist it into place. Blast them for 30 seconds. Put the rest of the solid ingredients into the cup and press them down below the Max Line. Add the fluid base to fill the cup up to the Max Line. Screw the Nutribullet Extractor Blade on to the top of the cup. Invert the cup, press it down into the Nutribullet Power Base and twist it into place. Blast the mixture until it is really smooth (20 or so seconds). **Enjoy!**

Strawberry embraces Tomato

Ingredients

1 Cup/Handful of Bok Choy (40 grams or 1½ oz)
1 Cup/Handful of Green Cabbage (40 grams or 1½ oz)
¾ Cup of Strawberries (90 grams or 3 oz)
1 Cup/Handful of sliced Tomato (120 grams or 4 oz)
22 grams or ¾ oz of Sesame Seeds Hulled
200 ml / 7 fl oz of Dairy Milk Whole

Protein 13g, Fat 21g, Carb 20g, Fibre 6g, 325 Kcals

Preparation

Place the nuts or seeds into the Tall Cup. Screw the Nutribullet Extractor Blade on to the top of the cup. Invert the cup, press it down into the Nutribullet Power Base and twist it into place. Blast them for 30 seconds. Put the rest of the solid ingredients into the cup and press them down below the Max Line. Add the fluid base to fill the cup up to the Max Line. Screw the Nutribullet Extractor Blade on to the top of the cup. Invert the cup, press it down into the Nutribullet Power Base and twist it into place. Blast the mixture until it is really smooth (20 or so seconds). **Enjoy!**

Radiant Skin Nourishing Blasts
High in Anti oxidants, Caroteinoids, Polyphenols, Pectin, Zinc, Vitamins A, C

Spinach and Pumpkin Adventure

Ingredients

2 Cups/Handfuls of Spinach (80 grams or 3 oz)
1½ Cups of Avocado slices (180 grams or 6 oz)
22 grams or ¾ oz of Pumpkin Seeds
100 ml / 3½ fl oz of Coconut Milk
100 ml / 3½ fl oz of Greek Yoghurt
Protein 15g, Fat 47g, Carb 15g, Fibre 15g, 575 Kcals

Preparation

Place the nuts or seeds into the Tall Cup. Screw the Nutribullet Extractor Blade on to the top of the cup. Invert the cup, press it down into the Nutribullet Power Base and twist it into place. Blast them for 30 seconds. Put the rest of the solid ingredients into the cup and press them down below the Max Line. Add the fluid base to fill the cup up to the Max Line. Screw the Nutribullet Extractor Blade on to the top of the cup. Invert the cup, press it down into the Nutribullet Power Base and twist it into place. Blast the mixture until it is really smooth (20 or so seconds). *Enjoy!*

Green Cabbage needs Blackberry

Ingredients

1 Cup/Handful of Rocket/Arugura Lettuce (40 grams or 1½ oz)
1 Cup/Handful of Green Cabbage (40 grams or 1½ oz)
¾ Cup of Avocado slices (90 grams or 3 oz)
¾ Cup of Blackberries (90 grams or 3 oz)
22 grams or ¾ oz of Pumpkin Seeds
100 ml / 3½ fl oz of Almond Milk (Unsweetened)
100 ml / 3½ fl oz of Greek Yoghurt
Protein 14g, Fat 34g, Carb 15g, Fibre 14g, 461 Kcals

Preparation

Place the nuts or seeds into the Tall Cup. Screw the Nutribullet Extractor Blade on to the top of the cup. Invert the cup, press it down into the Nutribullet Power Base and twist it into place. Blast them for 30 seconds. Put the rest of the solid ingredients into the cup and press them down below the Max Line. Add the fluid base to fill the cup up to the Max Line. Screw the Nutribullet Extractor Blade on to the top of the cup. Invert the cup, press it down into the Nutribullet Power Base and twist it into place. Blast the mixture until it is really smooth (20 or so seconds). *Enjoy!*

Green Cabbage and Pumpkin Recovery

Ingredients

1 Cup/Handful of Green Cabbage (40 grams or 1½ oz)
1 Cup/Handful of Rocket/Arugura Lettuce (40 grams or 1½ oz)
1½ Cups of Avocado slices (180 grams or 6 oz)
22 grams or ¾ oz of Pumpkin Seeds
100 ml / 3½ fl oz of Coconut Milk
100 ml / 3½ fl oz of Greek Yoghurt

Protein 14g, Fat 47g, Carb 16g, Fibre 15g, 573 Kcals

Preparation

Place the nuts or seeds into the Tall Cup. Screw the Nutribullet Extractor Blade on to the top of the cup. Invert the cup, press it down into the Nutribullet Power Base and twist it into place. Blast them for 30 seconds. Put the rest of the solid ingredients into the cup and press them down below the Max Line. Add the fluid base to fill the cup up to the Max Line. Screw the Nutribullet Extractor Blade on to the top of the cup. Invert the cup, press it down into the Nutribullet Power Base and twist it into place. Blast the mixture until it is really smooth (20 or so seconds). **Enjoy!**

Blackberry and Avocado Rapture

Ingredients

1 Cup/Handful of Mint (40 grams or 1½ oz)
1 Cup/Handful of Green Cabbage (40 grams or 1½ oz)
¾ Cup of Blackberries (90 grams or 3 oz)
¾ Cup of Avocado slices (90 grams or 3 oz)
22 grams or ¾ oz of Sesame Seeds Hulled
100 ml / 3½ fl oz of Hazelnut Milk
100 ml / 3½ fl oz of Greek Yoghurt

Protein 13g, Fat 38g, Carb 16g, Fibre 17g, 495 Kcals

Preparation

Place the nuts or seeds into the Tall Cup. Screw the Nutribullet Extractor Blade on to the top of the cup. Invert the cup, press it down into the Nutribullet Power Base and twist it into place. Blast them for 30 seconds. Put the rest of the solid ingredients into the cup and press them down below the Max Line. Add the fluid base to fill the cup up to the Max Line. Screw the Nutribullet Extractor Blade on to the top of the cup. Invert the cup, press it down into the Nutribullet Power Base and twist it into place. Blast the mixture until it is really smooth (20 or so seconds). **Enjoy!**

Strawberry Smash

Ingredients

2 Cups/Handfuls of Mint (80 grams or 3 oz)
¾ Cup of Avocado slices (90 grams or 3 oz)
¾ Cup of Strawberries (90 grams or 3 oz)
22 grams or ¾ oz of Sesame Seeds Hulled
100 ml / 3½ fl oz of Coconut Milk
100 ml / 3½ fl oz of Greek Yoghurt

Protein 13g, Fat 37g, Carb 16g, Fibre 15g, 484 Kcals

Preparation

Place the nuts or seeds into the Tall Cup. Screw the Nutribullet Extractor Blade on to the top of the cup. Invert the cup, press it down into the Nutribullet Power Base and twist it into place. Blast them for 30 seconds. Put the rest of the solid ingredients into the cup and press them down below the Max Line. Add the fluid base to fill the cup up to the Max Line. Screw the Nutribullet Extractor Blade on to the top of the cup. Invert the cup, press it down into the Nutribullet Power Base and twist it into place. Blast the mixture until it is really smooth (20 or so seconds). **Enjoy!**

Watercress on Blackberry

Ingredients

1 Cup/Handful of Black Kale de-stemmed (40 grams or 1½ oz)
1 Cup/Handful of Watercress (40 grams or 1½ oz)
1½ Cups of Blackberries (180 grams or 6 oz)
22 grams or ¾ oz of Pumpkin Seeds
100 ml / 3½ fl oz of Almond Milk (Unsweetened)
100 ml / 3½ fl oz of Greek Yoghurt

Protein 15g, Fat 22g, Carb 17g, Fibre 12g, 358 Kcals

Preparation

Place the nuts or seeds into the Tall Cup. Screw the Nutribullet Extractor Blade on to the top of the cup. Invert the cup, press it down into the Nutribullet Power Base and twist it into place. Blast them for 30 seconds. Put the rest of the solid ingredients into the cup and press them down below the Max Line. Add the fluid base to fill the cup up to the Max Line. Screw the Nutribullet Extractor Blade on to the top of the cup. Invert the cup, press it down into the Nutribullet Power Base and twist it into place. Blast the mixture until it is really smooth (20 or so seconds). **Enjoy!**

Bok Choy goes Pumpkin

Ingredients

1 Cup/Handful of Green Cabbage (40 grams or 1½ oz)
1 Cup/Handful of Bok Choy (40 grams or 1½ oz)
1½ Cups of Blackberries (180 grams or 6 oz)
22 grams or ¾ oz of Pumpkin Seeds
100 ml / 3½ fl oz of Almond Milk (Unsweetened)
100 ml / 3½ fl oz of Greek Yoghurt

Protein 13g, Fat 21g, Carb 17g, Fibre 13g, 354 Kcals

Preparation

Place the nuts or seeds into the Tall Cup. Screw the Nutribullet Extractor Blade on to the top of the cup. Invert the cup, press it down into the Nutribullet Power Base and twist it into place. Blast them for 30 seconds. Put the rest of the solid ingredients into the cup and press them down below the Max Line. Add the fluid base to fill the cup up to the Max Line. Screw the Nutribullet Extractor Blade on to the top of the cup. Invert the cup, press it down into the Nutribullet Power Base and twist it into place. Blast the mixture until it is really smooth (20 or so seconds). **Enjoy!**

Bok Choy and Black Kale Delusion

Ingredients

1 Cup/Handful of Bok Choy (40 grams or 1½ oz)
1 Cup/Handful of Black Kale de-stemmed (40 grams or 1½ oz)
¾ Cup of Peach slices (90 grams or 3 oz)
¾ Cup of Avocado slices (90 grams or 3 oz)
22 grams or ¾ oz of Pumpkin Seeds
100 ml / 3½ fl oz of Almond Milk (Unsweetened)
100 ml / 3½ fl oz of Greek Yoghurt

Protein 14g, Fat 34g, Carb 18g, Fibre 10g, 460 Kcals

Preparation

Place the nuts or seeds into the Tall Cup. Screw the Nutribullet Extractor Blade on to the top of the cup. Invert the cup, press it down into the Nutribullet Power Base and twist it into place. Blast them for 30 seconds. Put the rest of the solid ingredients into the cup and press them down below the Max Line. Add the fluid base to fill the cup up to the Max Line. Screw the Nutribullet Extractor Blade on to the top of the cup. Invert the cup, press it down into the Nutribullet Power Base and twist it into place. Blast the mixture until it is really smooth (20 or so seconds). **Enjoy!**

Mint embraces Raspberry

Ingredients

2 Cups/Handfuls of Mint (80 grams or 3 oz)
1½ Cups of Raspberries (180 grams or 6 oz)
22 grams or ¾ oz of Pumpkin Seeds
100 ml / 3½ fl oz of Almond Milk (Unsweetened)
100 ml / 3½ fl oz of Greek Yoghurt

Protein 15g, Fat 22g, Carb 19g, Fibre 19g, 391 Kcals

Preparation

Place the nuts or seeds into the Tall Cup. Screw the Nutribullet Extractor Blade on to the top of the cup. Invert the cup, press it down into the Nutribullet Power Base and twist it into place. Blast them for 30 seconds. Put the rest of the solid ingredients into the cup and press them down below the Max Line. Add the fluid base to fill the cup up to the Max Line. Screw the Nutribullet Extractor Blade on to the top of the cup. Invert the cup, press it down into the Nutribullet Power Base and twist it into place. Blast the mixture until it is really smooth (20 or so seconds). **Enjoy!**

Strawberry and Sesame Paradox

Ingredients

1 Cup/Handful of Rocket/Arugura Lettuce (40 grams or 1½ oz)
1 Cup/Handful of Black Kale de-stemmed (40 grams or 1½ oz)
1½ Cups of Strawberries (180 grams or 6 oz)
22 grams or ¾ oz of Sesame Seeds Hulled
100 ml / 3½ fl oz of Coconut Milk
100 ml / 3½ fl oz of Greek Yoghurt

Protein 11g, Fat 24g, Carb 20g, Fibre 7g, 354 Kcals

Preparation

Place the nuts or seeds into the Tall Cup. Screw the Nutribullet Extractor Blade on to the top of the cup. Invert the cup, press it down into the Nutribullet Power Base and twist it into place. Blast them for 30 seconds. Put the rest of the solid ingredients into the cup and press them down below the Max Line. Add the fluid base to fill the cup up to the Max Line. Screw the Nutribullet Extractor Blade on to the top of the cup. Invert the cup, press it down into the Nutribullet Power Base and twist it into place. Blast the mixture until it is really smooth (20 or so seconds). **Enjoy!**

Radiant Skin Nourishing Smoothies
High in Anti oxidants, Caroteinoids, Polyphenols, Pectin, Zinc, Vitamins A, C

Rocket goes Avocado

Ingredients

2 Cups/Handfuls of Rocket/Arugura Lettuce (80 grams or 3 oz)
1½ Cups of Avocado slices (180 grams or 6 oz)
100 ml / 3½ fl oz of Almond Milk (Unsweetened)
100 ml / 3½ fl oz of Greek Yoghurt

Protein 9g, Fat 37g, Carb 10g, Fibre 14g, 438 Kcals

Preparation

Put all the solid ingredients into the Tall Cup and press them down below the Max Line. Add the fluid base to fill the cup up to the Max Line. Screw the Nutribullet Extractor Blade on to the top of the cup. Invert the cup, press it down into the Nutribullet Power Base and twist it into place. Blast the mixture until it is really smooth (20 or so seconds). **Enjoy!**

Green Cabbage and Spinach Rocker

Ingredients

1 Cup/Handful of Green Cabbage (40 grams or 1½ oz)
1 Cup/Handful of Spinach (40 grams or 1½ oz)
1½ Cups of Avocado slices (180 grams or 6 oz)
100 ml / 3½ fl oz of Almond Milk (Unsweetened)
100 ml / 3½ fl oz of Greek Yoghurt

Protein 10g, Fat 37g, Carb 11g, Fibre 14g, 445 Kcals

Preparation

Put all the solid ingredients into the Tall Cup and press them down below the Max Line. Add the fluid base to fill the cup up to the Max Line. Screw the Nutribullet Extractor Blade on to the top of the cup. Invert the cup, press it down into the Nutribullet Power Base and twist it into place. Blast the mixture until it is really smooth (20 or so seconds). **Enjoy!**

Avocado and Peach Heaven

Ingredients

1 Cup/Handful of Black Kale de-stemmed (40 grams or 1½ oz)
1 Cup/Handful of Rocket/Arugura Lettuce (40 grams or 1½ oz)
¾ Cup of Avocado slices (90 grams or 3 oz)
¾ Cup of Peach slices (90 grams or 3 oz)
100 ml / 3½ fl oz of Almond Milk (Unsweetened)
100 ml / 3½ fl oz of Greek Yoghurt

Protein 9g, Fat 25g, Carb 16g, Fibre 9g, 337 Kcals

Preparation

Put all the solid ingredients into the Tall Cup and press them down below the Max Line. Add the fluid base to fill the cup up to the Max Line. Screw the Nutribullet Extractor Blade on to the top of the cup. Invert the cup, press it down into the Nutribullet Power Base and twist it into place. Blast the mixture until it is really smooth (20 or so seconds). **Enjoy!**

Strawberry and Avocado Panacea

Ingredients

2 Cups/Handfuls of Bok Choy (80 grams or 3 oz)
¾ Cup of Strawberries (90 grams or 3 oz)
¾ Cup of Avocado slices (90 grams or 3 oz)
100 ml / 3½ fl oz of Coconut Milk
100 ml / 3½ fl oz of Greek Yoghurt

Protein 8g, Fat 24g, Carb 16g, Fibre 9g, 328 Kcals

Preparation

Put all the solid ingredients into the Tall Cup and press them down below the Max Line. Add the fluid base to fill the cup up to the Max Line. Screw the Nutribullet Extractor Blade on to the top of the cup. Invert the cup, press it down into the Nutribullet Power Base and twist it into place. Blast the mixture until it is really smooth (20 or so seconds). **Enjoy!**

Mint needs Blackberry

Ingredients

1 Cup/Handful of Black Kale de-stemmed (40 grams or 1½ oz)
1 Cup/Handful of Mint (40 grams or 1½ oz)
¾ Cup of Avocado slices (90 grams or 3 oz)
¾ Cup of Blackberries (90 grams or 3 oz)
200 ml / 7 fl oz of Dairy Milk Semi Skimmed

Protein 13g, Fat 18g, Carb 16g, Fibre 14g, 314 Kcals

Preparation

Put all the solid ingredients into the Tall Cup and press them down below the Max Line. Add the fluid base to fill the cup up to the Max Line. Screw the Nutribullet Extractor Blade on to the top of the cup. Invert the cup, press it down into the Nutribullet Power Base and twist it into place. Blast the mixture until it is really smooth (20 or so seconds). ***Enjoy!***

Cranberry Cocktail

Ingredients

1 Cup/Handful of Rocket/Arugura Lettuce (40 grams or 1½ oz)
1 Cup/Handful of Bok Choy (40 grams or 1½ oz)
¾ Cup of Raspberries (90 grams or 3 oz)
¾ Cup of Cranberries (90 grams or 3 oz)
100 ml / 3½ fl oz of Almond Milk (Unsweetened)
100 ml / 3½ fl oz of Greek Yoghurt

Protein 7g, Fat 11g, Carb 18g, Fibre 11g, 237 Kcals

Preparation

Put all the solid ingredients into the Tall Cup and press them down below the Max Line. Add the fluid base to fill the cup up to the Max Line. Screw the Nutribullet Extractor Blade on to the top of the cup. Invert the cup, press it down into the Nutribullet Power Base and twist it into place. Blast the mixture until it is really smooth (20 or so seconds). ***Enjoy!***

Mint in Peach

Ingredients

1 Cup/Handful of Rocket/Arugura Lettuce (40 grams or 1½ oz)
1 Cup/Handful of Mint (40 grams or 1½ oz)
¾ Cup of Avocado slices (90 grams or 3 oz)
¾ Cup of Peach slices (90 grams or 3 oz)
100 ml / 3½ fl oz of Hazelnut Milk
100 ml / 3½ fl oz of Greek Yoghurt

Protein 9g, Fat 25g, Carb 19g, Fibre 11g, 356 Kcals

Preparation

Put all the solid ingredients into the Tall Cup and press them down below the Max Line. Add the fluid base to fill the cup up to the Max Line. Screw the Nutribullet Extractor Blade on to the top of the cup. Invert the cup, press it down into the Nutribullet Power Base and twist it into place. Blast the mixture until it is really smooth (20 or so seconds). **Enjoy!**

Black Kale joins Blackberry

Ingredients

2 Cups/Handfuls of Black Kale de-stemmed (80 grams or 3 oz)
1½ Cups of Blackberries (180 grams or 6 oz)
200 ml / 7 fl oz of Dairy Milk Semi Skimmed

Protein 12g, Fat 6g, Carb 19g, Fibre 11g, 205 Kcals

Preparation

Put all the solid ingredients into the Tall Cup and press them down below the Max Line. Add the fluid base to fill the cup up to the Max Line. Screw the Nutribullet Extractor Blade on to the top of the cup. Invert the cup, press it down into the Nutribullet Power Base and twist it into place. Blast the mixture until it is really smooth (20 or so seconds). **Enjoy!**

Black Kale meets Avocado

Ingredients

1 Cup/Handful of Green Cabbage (40 grams or 1½ oz)
1 Cup/Handful of Black Kale de-stemmed (40 grams or 1½ oz)
¾ Cup of Cranberries (90 grams or 3 oz)
¾ Cup of Avocado slices (90 grams or 3 oz)
100 ml / 3½ fl oz of Hazelnut Milk
100 ml / 3½ fl oz of Greek Yoghurt

Protein 9g, Fat 25g, Carb 19g, Fibre 12g, 363 Kcals

Preparation

Put all the solid ingredients into the Tall Cup and press them down below the Max Line. Add the fluid base to fill the cup up to the Max Line. Screw the Nutribullet Extractor Blade on to the top of the cup. Invert the cup, press it down into the Nutribullet Power Base and twist it into place. Blast the mixture until it is really smooth (20 or so seconds). **Enjoy!**

Rocket on Plum

Ingredients

1 Cup/Handful of Watercress (40 grams or 1½ oz)
1 Cup/Handful of Rocket/Arugura Lettuce (40 grams or 1½ oz)
¾ Cup of Plum halves (90 grams or 3 oz)
¾ Cup of Blackberries (90 grams or 3 oz)
100 ml / 3½ fl oz of Almond Milk (Unsweetened)
100 ml / 3½ fl oz of Greek Yoghurt

Protein 8g, Fat 11g, Carb 19g, Fibre 7g, 228 Kcals

Preparation

Put all the solid ingredients into the Tall Cup and press them down below the Max Line. Add the fluid base to fill the cup up to the Max Line. Screw the Nutribullet Extractor Blade on to the top of the cup. Invert the cup, press it down into the Nutribullet Power Base and twist it into place. Blast the mixture until it is really smooth (20 or so seconds). **Enjoy!**

Blackberry loves Pecan

Ingredients

1½ Cups of Blackberries (180 grams or 6 oz)
30 grams or 1 oz of Pecans
200 ml / 7 fl oz of Coconut Milk

Protein 5g, Fat 24g, Carb 14g, Fibre 12g, 324 Kcals

Preparation

Place the nuts or seeds into the Tall Cup. Screw the Nutribullet Extractor Blade on to the top of the cup. Invert the cup, press it down into the Nutribullet Power Base and twist it into place. Blast them for 30 seconds. Put the rest of the solid ingredients into the cup and press them down below the Max Line. Add the fluid base to fill the cup up to the Max Line. Screw the Nutribullet Extractor Blade on to the top of the cup. Invert the cup, press it down into the Nutribullet Power Base and twist it into place. Blast the mixture until it is really smooth (20 or so seconds). *Enjoy!*

Strawberry on Peanut

Ingredients

¾ Cup of Blackberries (90 grams or 3 oz)
¾ Cup of Strawberries (90 grams or 3 oz)
30 grams or 1 oz of Peanuts
200 ml / 7 fl oz of Hazelnut Milk

Protein 10g, Fat 19g, Carb 17g, Fibre 10g, 295 Kcals

Preparation

Place the nuts or seeds into the Tall Cup. Screw the Nutribullet Extractor Blade on to the top of the cup. Invert the cup, press it down into the Nutribullet Power Base and twist it into place. Blast them for 30 seconds. Put the rest of the solid ingredients into the cup and press them down below the Max Line. Add the fluid base to fill the cup up to the Max Line. Screw the Nutribullet Extractor Blade on to the top of the cup. Invert the cup, press it down into the Nutribullet Power Base and twist it into place. Blast the mixture until it is really smooth (20 or so seconds). *Enjoy!*

Strawberry and Peanut Perfection

Ingredients

1½ Cups of Strawberries (180 grams or 6 oz)
30 grams or 1 oz of Peanuts
200 ml / 7 fl oz of Coconut Milk

Protein 9g, Fat 17g, Carb 18g, Fibre 6g, 267 Kcals

Preparation

Place the nuts or seeds into the Tall Cup. Screw the Nutribullet Extractor Blade on to the top of the cup. Invert the cup, press it down into the Nutribullet Power Base and twist it into place. Blast them for 30 seconds. Put the rest of the solid ingredients into the cup and press them down below the Max Line. Add the fluid base to fill the cup up to the Max Line. Screw the Nutribullet Extractor Blade on to the top of the cup. Invert the cup, press it down into the Nutribullet Power Base and twist it into place. Blast the mixture until it is really smooth (20 or so seconds). **Enjoy!**

Water Melon goes Blackberry

Ingredients

¾ Cup of Water Melon chunks (90 grams or 3 oz)
¾ Cup of Blackberries (90 grams or 3 oz)
30 grams or 1 oz of Peanuts
200 ml / 7 fl oz of Coconut Milk

Protein 10g, Fat 17g, Carb 18g, Fibre 8g, 275 Kcals

Preparation

Place the nuts or seeds into the Tall Cup. Screw the Nutribullet Extractor Blade on to the top of the cup. Invert the cup, press it down into the Nutribullet Power Base and twist it into place. Blast them for 30 seconds. Put the rest of the solid ingredients into the cup and press them down below the Max Line. Add the fluid base to fill the cup up to the Max Line. Screw the Nutribullet Extractor Blade on to the top of the cup. Invert the cup, press it down into the Nutribullet Power Base and twist it into place. Blast the mixture until it is really smooth (20 or so seconds). **Enjoy!**

Cranberry and Almond Forever

Ingredients

¾ Cup of Blackberries (90 grams or 3 oz)
¾ Cup of Cranberries (90 grams or 3 oz)
30 grams or 1 oz of Almonds
200 ml / 7 fl oz of Coconut Milk

Protein 8g, Fat 18g, Carb 18g, Fibre 12g, 297 Kcals

Preparation

Place the nuts or seeds into the Tall Cup. Screw the Nutribullet Extractor Blade on to the top of the cup. Invert the cup, press it down into the Nutribullet Power Base and twist it into place. Blast them for 30 seconds. Put the rest of the solid ingredients into the cup and press them down below the Max Line. Add the fluid base to fill the cup up to the Max Line. Screw the Nutribullet Extractor Blade on to the top of the cup. Invert the cup, press it down into the Nutribullet Power Base and twist it into place. Blast the mixture until it is really smooth (20 or so seconds). **Enjoy!**

Peach and Pecan Avarice

Ingredients

¾ Cup of Blackberries (90 grams or 3 oz)
¾ Cup of Peach slices (90 grams or 3 oz)
30 grams or 1 oz of Pecans
200 ml / 7 fl oz of Hazelnut Milk

Protein 5g, Fat 25g, Carb 18g, Fibre 10g, 339 Kcals

Preparation

Place the nuts or seeds into the Tall Cup. Screw the Nutribullet Extractor Blade on to the top of the cup. Invert the cup, press it down into the Nutribullet Power Base and twist it into place. Blast them for 30 seconds. Put the rest of the solid ingredients into the cup and press them down below the Max Line. Add the fluid base to fill the cup up to the Max Line. Screw the Nutribullet Extractor Blade on to the top of the cup. Invert the cup, press it down into the Nutribullet Power Base and twist it into place. Blast the mixture until it is really smooth (20 or so seconds). **Enjoy!**

Nectarine and Blackberry Sensation

Ingredients

¾ Cup of Nectarine segments (90 grams or 3 oz)
¾ Cup of Blackberries (90 grams or 3 oz)
30 grams or 1 oz of Brazil nuts
200 ml / 7 fl oz of Coconut Milk

Protein 7g, Fat 23g, Carb 19g, Fibre 9g, 315 Kcals

Preparation

Place the nuts or seeds into the Tall Cup. Screw the Nutribullet Extractor Blade on to the top of the cup. Invert the cup, press it down into the Nutribullet Power Base and twist it into place. Blast them for 30 seconds. Put the rest of the solid ingredients into the cup and press them down below the Max Line. Add the fluid base to fill the cup up to the Max Line. Screw the Nutribullet Extractor Blade on to the top of the cup. Invert the cup, press it down into the Nutribullet Power Base and twist it into place. Blast the mixture until it is really smooth (20 or so seconds). *Enjoy!*

Raspberry meets Walnut

Ingredients

¾ Cup of Water Melon chunks (90 grams or 3 oz)
¾ Cup of Raspberries (90 grams or 3 oz)
30 grams or 1 oz of Walnuts
200 ml / 7 fl oz of Hazelnut Milk

Protein 7g, Fat 23g, Carb 19g, Fibre 9g, 327 Kcals

Preparation

Place the nuts or seeds into the Tall Cup. Screw the Nutribullet Extractor Blade on to the top of the cup. Invert the cup, press it down into the Nutribullet Power Base and twist it into place. Blast them for 30 seconds. Put the rest of the solid ingredients into the cup and press them down below the Max Line. Add the fluid base to fill the cup up to the Max Line. Screw the Nutribullet Extractor Blade on to the top of the cup. Invert the cup, press it down into the Nutribullet Power Base and twist it into place. Blast the mixture until it is really smooth (20 or so seconds). *Enjoy!*

Brazil Bonanza

Ingredients

1½ Cups of Grapefruit segments (180 grams or 6 oz)
30 grams or 1 oz of Brazil nuts
100 ml / 3½ fl oz of Almond Milk (Unsweetened)
100 ml / 3½ fl oz of Greek Yoghurt

Protein 10g, Fat 31g, Carb 19g, Fibre 5g, 393 Kcals

Preparation

Place the nuts or seeds into the Tall Cup. Screw the Nutribullet Extractor Blade on to the top of the cup. Invert the cup, press it down into the Nutribullet Power Base and twist it into place. Blast them for 30 seconds. Put the rest of the solid ingredients into the cup and press them down below the Max Line. Add the fluid base to fill the cup up to the Max Line. Screw the Nutribullet Extractor Blade on to the top of the cup. Invert the cup, press it down into the Nutribullet Power Base and twist it into place. Blast the mixture until it is really smooth (20 or so seconds). **Enjoy!**

Water Melon loves Pecan

Ingredients

1½ Cups of Water Melon chunks (180 grams or 8 oz)
30 grams or 1 oz of Pecans
200 ml / 7 fl oz of Coconut Milk

Protein 4g, Fat 24g, Carb 20g, Fibre 4g, 301 Kcals

Preparation

Place the nuts or seeds into the Tall Cup. Screw the Nutribullet Extractor Blade on to the top of the cup. Invert the cup, press it down into the Nutribullet Power Base and twist it into place. Blast them for 30 seconds. Put the rest of the solid ingredients into the cup and press them down below the Max Line. Add the fluid base to fill the cup up to the Max Line. Screw the Nutribullet Extractor Blade on to the top of the cup. Invert the cup, press it down into the Nutribullet Power Base and twist it into place. Blast the mixture until it is really smooth (20 or so seconds). **Enjoy!**

Classic Low Carb Blasts - *All less than 20 Carb grams*

Blackberry and Brazil Feast

Ingredients

1 Cup/Handful of Fennel (40 grams or 1½ oz)
1 Cup/Handful of Bok Choy (40 grams or 1½ oz)
¾ Cup of Blackberries (90 grams or 3 oz)
1 Cup/Handful of sliced Celery (120 grams or 4 oz)
30 grams or 1 oz of Brazil nuts
200 ml / 7 fl oz of Almond Milk (Unsweetened)

Protein 8g, Fat 23g, Carb 9g, Fibre 11g, 299 Kcals

Preparation

Place the nuts or seeds into the Tall Cup. Screw the Nutribullet Extractor Blade on to the top of the cup. Invert the cup, press it down into the Nutribullet Power Base and twist it into place. Blast them for 30 seconds. Put the rest of the solid ingredients into the cup and press them down below the Max Line. Add the fluid base to fill the cup up to the Max Line. Screw the Nutribullet Extractor Blade on to the top of the cup. Invert the cup, press it down into the Nutribullet Power Base and twist it into place. Blast the mixture until it is really smooth (20 or so seconds). *Enjoy!*

Green Pepper Garden

Ingredients

2 Cups/Handfuls of Rocket/Arugura Lettuce (80 grams or 3 oz)
¾ Cup of Blackberries (90 grams or 3 oz)
1 Cup/Handful of sliced Green Pepper (120 grams or 4 oz)
30 grams or 1 oz of Pecans
200 ml / 7 fl oz of Almond Milk (Unsweetened)

Protein 7g, Fat 25g, Carb 10g, Fibre 12g, 307 Kcals

Preparation

Place the nuts or seeds into the Tall Cup. Screw the Nutribullet Extractor Blade on to the top of the cup. Invert the cup, press it down into the Nutribullet Power Base and twist it into place. Blast them for 30 seconds. Put the rest of the solid ingredients into the cup and press them down below the Max Line. Add the fluid base to fill the cup up to the Max Line. Screw the Nutribullet Extractor Blade on to the top of the cup. Invert the cup, press it down into the Nutribullet Power Base and twist it into place. Blast the mixture until it is really smooth (20 or so seconds). *Enjoy!*

Grapefruit and Brazil Ensemble

Ingredients

1 Cup/Handful of Watercress (40 grams or 1½ oz)
1 Cup/Handful of Rocket/Arugura Lettuce (40 grams or 1½ oz)
¾ Cup of Grapefruit segments (90 grams or 3 oz)
1 Cup/Handful of sliced Tomato (120 grams or 4 oz)
30 grams or 1 oz of Brazil nuts
200 ml / 7 fl oz of Almond Milk (Unsweetened)

Protein 8g, Fat 23g, Carb 12g, Fibre 6g, 284 Kcals

Preparation

Place the nuts or seeds into the Tall Cup. Screw the Nutribullet Extractor Blade on to the top of the cup. Invert the cup, press it down into the Nutribullet Power Base and twist it into place. Blast them for 30 seconds. Put the rest of the solid ingredients into the cup and press them down below the Max Line. Add the fluid base to fill the cup up to the Max Line. Screw the Nutribullet Extractor Blade on to the top of the cup. Invert the cup, press it down into the Nutribullet Power Base and twist it into place. Blast the mixture until it is really smooth (20 or so seconds). **Enjoy!**

Walnut Wonder

Ingredients

1 Cup/Handful of Watercress (40 grams or 1½ oz)
1 Cup/Handful of Green Cabbage (40 grams or 1½ oz)
¾ Cup of Raspberries (90 grams or 3 oz)
1 Cup/Handful of sliced Fine Beans (120 grams or 4 oz)
30 grams or 1 oz of Walnuts
200 ml / 7 fl oz of Almond Milk (Unsweetened)

Protein 10g, Fat 23g, Carb 13g, Fibre 13g, 313 Kcals

Preparation

Place the nuts or seeds into the Tall Cup. Screw the Nutribullet Extractor Blade on to the top of the cup. Invert the cup, press it down into the Nutribullet Power Base and twist it into place. Blast them for 30 seconds. Put the rest of the solid ingredients into the cup and press them down below the Max Line. Add the fluid base to fill the cup up to the Max Line. Screw the Nutribullet Extractor Blade on to the top of the cup. Invert the cup, press it down into the Nutribullet Power Base and twist it into place. Blast the mixture until it is really smooth (20 or so seconds). **Enjoy!**

Green Extravaganza

Ingredients

2 Cups/Handfuls of Green Cabbage (80 grams or 3 oz)
¾ Cup of Blackberries (90 grams or 3 oz)
1 Cup/Handful of sliced Red Pepper (120 grams or 4 oz)
30 grams or 1 oz of Walnuts
200 ml / 7 fl oz of Almond Milk (Unsweetened)

Protein 9g, Fat 23g, Carb 14g, Fibre 12g, 318 Kcals

Preparation

Place the nuts or seeds into the Tall Cup. Screw the Nutribullet Extractor Blade on to the top of the cup. Invert the cup, press it down into the Nutribullet Power Base and twist it into place. Blast them for 30 seconds. Put the rest of the solid ingredients into the cup and press them down below the Max Line. Add the fluid base to fill the cup up to the Max Line. Screw the Nutribullet Extractor Blade on to the top of the cup. Invert the cup, press it down into the Nutribullet Power Base and twist it into place. Blast the mixture until it is really smooth (20 or so seconds). **Enjoy!**

Fennel and Clementine Snog

Ingredients

1 Cup/Handful of Fennel (40 grams or 1½ oz)
1 Cup/Handful of Bok Choy (40 grams or 1½ oz)
¾ Cup of Clementine slices (90 grams or 3 oz)
1 Cup/Handful of sliced Cucumber (120 grams or 4 oz)
30 grams or 1 oz of Almonds
200 ml / 7 fl oz of Almond Milk (Unsweetened)

Protein 10g, Fat 19g, Carb 15g, Fibre 8g, 277 Kcals

Preparation

Place the nuts or seeds into the Tall Cup. Screw the Nutribullet Extractor Blade on to the top of the cup. Invert the cup, press it down into the Nutribullet Power Base and twist it into place. Blast them for 30 seconds. Put the rest of the solid ingredients into the cup and press them down below the Max Line. Add the fluid base to fill the cup up to the Max Line. Screw the Nutribullet Extractor Blade on to the top of the cup. Invert the cup, press it down into the Nutribullet Power Base and twist it into place. Blast the mixture until it is really smooth (20 or so seconds). **Enjoy!**

Fennel embraces Brazil

Ingredients

1 Cup/Handful of Fennel (40 grams or 1½ oz)
1 Cup/Handful of Lettuce Leaves (40 grams or 1½ oz)
¾ Cup of Orange segments (90 grams or 3 oz)
1 Cup/Handful of sliced Cauliflower florets (120 grams or 4 oz)
30 grams or 1 oz of Brazil nuts
200 ml / 7 fl oz of Almond Milk (Unsweetened)

Protein 9g, Fat 23g, Carb 16g, Fibre 10g, 315 Kcals

Preparation

Place the nuts or seeds into the Tall Cup. Screw the Nutribullet Extractor Blade on to the top of the cup. Invert the cup, press it down into the Nutribullet Power Base and twist it into place. Blast them for 30 seconds. Put the rest of the solid ingredients into the cup and press them down below the Max Line. Add the fluid base to fill the cup up to the Max Line. Screw the Nutribullet Extractor Blade on to the top of the cup. Invert the cup, press it down into the Nutribullet Power Base and twist it into place. Blast the mixture until it is really smooth (20 or so seconds). **Enjoy!**

Cashew Collection

Ingredients

1 Cup/Handful of Broccoli Florets (40 grams or 1½ oz)
1 Cup/Handful of Green Cabbage (40 grams or 1½ oz)
¾ Cup of Avocado slices (90 grams or 3 oz)
1 Cup/Handful of sliced Tomato (120 grams or 4 oz)
30 grams or 1 oz of Cashews
200 ml / 7 fl oz of Almond Milk (Unsweetened)

Protein 11g, Fat 29g, Carb 16g, Fibre 11g, 381 Kcals

Preparation

Place the nuts or seeds into the Tall Cup. Screw the Nutribullet Extractor Blade on to the top of the cup. Invert the cup, press it down into the Nutribullet Power Base and twist it into place. Blast them for 30 seconds. Put the rest of the solid ingredients into the cup and press them down below the Max Line. Add the fluid base to fill the cup up to the Max Line. Screw the Nutribullet Extractor Blade on to the top of the cup. Invert the cup, press it down into the Nutribullet Power Base and twist it into place. Blast the mixture until it is really smooth (20 or so seconds). **Enjoy!**

Celery Chorus

Ingredients

1 Cup/Handful of Mint (40 grams or 1½ oz)
1 Cup/Handful of Red or White Cabbage (40 grams or 1½ oz)
¾ Cup of Avocado slices (90 grams or 3 oz)
1 Cup/Handful of sliced Celery (120 grams or 4 oz)
30 grams or 1 oz of Pecans
200 ml / 7 fl oz of Dairy Milk Whole

Protein 14g, Fat 43g, Carb 17g, Fibre 14g, 528 Kcals

Preparation

Place the nuts or seeds into the Tall Cup. Screw the Nutribullet Extractor Blade on to the top of the cup. Invert the cup, press it down into the Nutribullet Power Base and twist it into place. Blast them for 30 seconds. Put the rest of the solid ingredients into the cup and press them down below the Max Line. Add the fluid base to fill the cup up to the Max Line. Screw the Nutribullet Extractor Blade on to the top of the cup. Invert the cup, press it down into the Nutribullet Power Base and twist it into place. Blast the mixture until it is really smooth (20 or so seconds). **Enjoy!**

Red Cabbage in Brazil

Ingredients

1 Cup/Handful of Red or White Cabbage (40 grams or 1½ oz)
1 Cup/Handful of Watercress (40 grams or 1½ oz)
¾ Cup of Avocado slices (90 grams or 3 oz)
1 Cup/Handful of diced Turnip (120 grams or 4 oz)
30 grams or 1 oz of Brazil nuts
200 ml / 7 fl oz of Hazelnut Milk

Protein 9g, Fat 37g, Carb 17g, Fibre 12g, 450 Kcals

Preparation

Place the nuts or seeds into the Tall Cup. Screw the Nutribullet Extractor Blade on to the top of the cup. Invert the cup, press it down into the Nutribullet Power Base and twist it into place. Blast them for 30 seconds. Put the rest of the solid ingredients into the cup and press them down below the Max Line. Add the fluid base to fill the cup up to the Max Line. Screw the Nutribullet Extractor Blade on to the top of the cup. Invert the cup, press it down into the Nutribullet Power Base and twist it into place. Blast the mixture until it is really smooth (20 or so seconds). **Enjoy!**

Mint and Watercress Revelation

Ingredients

1 Cup/Handful of Mint (40 grams or 1½ oz)
1 Cup/Handful of Watercress (40 grams or 1½ oz)
¾ Cup of Blueberries (90 grams or 3 oz)
1 Cup/Handful of sliced Tomato (120 grams or 4 oz)
30 grams or 1 oz of Peanuts
200 ml / 7 fl oz of Almond Milk (Unsweetened)

Protein 12g, Fat 18g, Carb 18g, Fibre 10g, 291 Kcals

Preparation

Place the nuts or seeds into the Tall Cup. Screw the Nutribullet Extractor Blade on to the top of the cup. Invert the cup, press it down into the Nutribullet Power Base and twist it into place. Blast them for 30 seconds. Put the rest of the solid ingredients into the cup and press them down below the Max Line. Add the fluid base to fill the cup up to the Max Line. Screw the Nutribullet Extractor Blade on to the top of the cup. Invert the cup, press it down into the Nutribullet Power Base and twist it into place. Blast the mixture until it is really smooth (20 or so seconds). **Enjoy!**

Cherry Creation

Ingredients

1 Cup/Handful of Black Kale de-stemmed (40 grams or 1½ oz)
1 Cup/Handful of Fennel (40 grams or 1½ oz)
¾ Cup of Cherries (stoned) (90 grams or 3 oz)
1 Cup/Handful of sliced Celery (120 grams or 4 oz)
30 grams or 1 oz of Brazil nuts
200 ml / 7 fl oz of Almond Milk (Unsweetened)

Protein 9g, Fat 23g, Carb 18g, Fibre 9g, 325 Kcals

Preparation

Place the nuts or seeds into the Tall Cup. Screw the Nutribullet Extractor Blade on to the top of the cup. Invert the cup, press it down into the Nutribullet Power Base and twist it into place. Blast them for 30 seconds. Put the rest of the solid ingredients into the cup and press them down below the Max Line. Add the fluid base to fill the cup up to the Max Line. Screw the Nutribullet Extractor Blade on to the top of the cup. Invert the cup, press it down into the Nutribullet Power Base and twist it into place. Blast the mixture until it is really smooth (20 or so seconds). **Enjoy!**

Avocado needs Brazil

Ingredients

2 Cups/Handfuls of Mint (80 grams or 3 oz)
¾ Cup of Avocado slices (90 grams or 3 oz)
1 Cup/Handful of diced Turnip (120 grams or 4 oz)
30 grams or 1 oz of Brazil nuts
100 ml / 3½ fl oz of Hazelnut Milk
100 ml / 3½ fl oz of Greek Yoghurt

Protein 14g, Fat 45g, Carb 18g, Fibre 16g, 564 Kcals

Preparation

Place the nuts or seeds into the Tall Cup. Screw the Nutribullet Extractor Blade on to the top of the cup. Invert the cup, press it down into the Nutribullet Power Base and twist it into place. Blast them for 30 seconds. Put the rest of the solid ingredients into the cup and press them down below the Max Line. Add the fluid base to fill the cup up to the Max Line. Screw the Nutribullet Extractor Blade on to the top of the cup. Invert the cup, press it down into the Nutribullet Power Base and twist it into place. Blast the mixture until it is really smooth (20 or so seconds). **Enjoy!**

Mint and Blackberry Session

Ingredients

1 Cup/Handful of Rocket/Arugura Lettuce (40 grams or 1½ oz)
1 Cup/Handful of Mint (40 grams or 1½ oz)
¾ Cup of Blackberries (90 grams or 3 oz)
1 Cup/Handful of sliced Cucumber (120 grams or 4 oz)
30 grams or 1 oz of Hazelnuts
200 ml / 7 fl oz of Dairy Milk Whole

Protein 15g, Fat 26g, Carb 18g, Fibre 12g, 393 Kcals

Preparation

Place the nuts or seeds into the Tall Cup. Screw the Nutribullet Extractor Blade on to the top of the cup. Invert the cup, press it down into the Nutribullet Power Base and twist it into place. Blast them for 30 seconds. Put the rest of the solid ingredients into the cup and press them down below the Max Line. Add the fluid base to fill the cup up to the Max Line. Screw the Nutribullet Extractor Blade on to the top of the cup. Invert the cup, press it down into the Nutribullet Power Base and twist it into place. Blast the mixture until it is really smooth (20 or so seconds). **Enjoy!**

Bok Choy and Almond Rave

Ingredients

1 Cup/Handful of Bok Choy (40 grams or 1½ oz)
1 Cup/Handful of Fennel (40 grams or 1½ oz)
¾ Cup of Water Melon chunks (90 grams or 3 oz)
1 Cup/Handful of Radishes (120 grams or 4 oz)
30 grams or 1 oz of Almonds
100 ml / 3½ fl oz of Almond Milk (Unsweetened)
100 ml / 3½ fl oz of Greek Yoghurt

Protein 13g, Fat 27g, Carb 18g, Fibre 7g, 378 Kcals

Preparation

Place the nuts or seeds into the Tall Cup. Screw the Nutribullet Extractor Blade on to the top of the cup. Invert the cup, press it down into the Nutribullet Power Base and twist it into place. Blast them for 30 seconds. Put the rest of the solid ingredients into the cup and press them down below the Max Line. Add the fluid base to fill the cup up to the Max Line. Screw the Nutribullet Extractor Blade on to the top of the cup. Invert the cup, press it down into the Nutribullet Power Base and twist it into place. Blast the mixture until it is really smooth (20 or so seconds). *Enjoy!*

Bok Choy joins Blackberry

Ingredients

1 Cup/Handful of Broccoli Florets (40 grams or 1½ oz)
1 Cup/Handful of Bok Choy (40 grams or 1½ oz)
¾ Cup of Blackberries (90 grams or 3 oz)
1 Cup/Handful of sliced Asparagus (120 grams or 4 oz)
30 grams or 1 oz of Hazelnuts
100 ml / 3½ fl oz of Hazelnut Milk
100 ml / 3½ fl oz of Greek Yoghurt

Protein 15g, Fat 30g, Carb 19g, Fibre 12g, 423 Kcals

Preparation

Place the nuts or seeds into the Tall Cup. Screw the Nutribullet Extractor Blade on to the top of the cup. Invert the cup, press it down into the Nutribullet Power Base and twist it into place. Blast them for 30 seconds. Put the rest of the solid ingredients into the cup and press them down below the Max Line. Add the fluid base to fill the cup up to the Max Line. Screw the Nutribullet Extractor Blade on to the top of the cup. Invert the cup, press it down into the Nutribullet Power Base and twist it into place. Blast the mixture until it is really smooth (20 or so seconds). *Enjoy!*

Broccoli and Pecan Sunset

Ingredients

1 Cup/Handful of Mint (40 grams or 1½ oz)
1 Cup/Handful of Broccoli Florets (40 grams or 1½ oz)
¾ Cup of Guava (90 grams or 3 oz)
1 Cup/Handful of sliced Zucchini/Courgette (120 grams or 4 oz)
30 grams or 1 oz of Pecans
200 ml / 7 fl oz of Coconut Milk

Protein 9g, Fat 25g, Carb 19g, Fibre 13g, 360 Kcals

Preparation

Place the nuts or seeds into the Tall Cup. Screw the Nutribullet Extractor Blade on to the top of the cup. Invert the cup, press it down into the Nutribullet Power Base and twist it into place. Blast them for 30 seconds. Put the rest of the solid ingredients into the cup and press them down below the Max Line. Add the fluid base to fill the cup up to the Max Line. Screw the Nutribullet Extractor Blade on to the top of the cup. Invert the cup, press it down into the Nutribullet Power Base and twist it into place. Blast the mixture until it is really smooth (20 or so seconds). **Enjoy!**

Lettuce joins Raspberry

Ingredients

1 Cup/Handful of Lettuce Leaves (40 grams or 1½ oz)
1 Cup/Handful of Red or White Cabbage (40 grams or 1½ oz)
¾ Cup of Raspberries (90 grams or 3 oz)
1 Cup/Handful of sliced Asparagus (120 grams or 4 oz)
30 grams or 1 oz of Brazil nuts
100 ml / 3½ fl oz of Hazelnut Milk
100 ml / 3½ fl oz of Greek Yoghurt

Protein 14g, Fat 32g, Carb 20g, Fibre 12g, 441 Kcals

Preparation

Place the nuts or seeds into the Tall Cup. Screw the Nutribullet Extractor Blade on to the top of the cup. Invert the cup, press it down into the Nutribullet Power Base and twist it into place. Blast them for 30 seconds. Put the rest of the solid ingredients into the cup and press them down below the Max Line. Add the fluid base to fill the cup up to the Max Line. Screw the Nutribullet Extractor Blade on to the top of the cup. Invert the cup, press it down into the Nutribullet Power Base and twist it into place. Blast the mixture until it is really smooth (20 or so seconds). **Enjoy!**

Apple Paradise

Ingredients

1 Cup/Handful of Watercress (40 grams or 1½ oz)
1 Cup/Handful of Black Kale de-stemmed (40 grams or 1½ oz)
¾ Cup of Apple slices (90 grams or 3 oz)
1 Cup/Handful of sliced Cucumber (120 grams or 4 oz)
30 grams or 1 oz of Brazil nuts
100 ml / 3½ fl oz of Almond Milk (Unsweetened)
100 ml / 3½ fl oz of Greek Yoghurt

Protein 12g, Fat 32g, Carb 20g, Fibre 7g, 415 Kcals

Preparation

Place the nuts or seeds into the Tall Cup. Screw the Nutribullet Extractor Blade on to the top of the cup. Invert the cup, press it down into the Nutribullet Power Base and twist it into place. Blast them for 30 seconds. Put the rest of the solid ingredients into the cup and press them down below the Max Line. Add the fluid base to fill the cup up to the Max Line. Screw the Nutribullet Extractor Blade on to the top of the cup. Invert the cup, press it down into the Nutribullet Power Base and twist it into place. Blast the mixture until it is really smooth (20 or so seconds). *Enjoy!*

Melon meets Red Pepper

Ingredients

1 Cup/Handful of Lettuce Leaves (40 grams or 1½ oz)
1 Cup/Handful of Mint (40 grams or 1½ oz)
¾ Cup of Melon chunks (90 grams or 3 oz)
1 Cup/Handful of sliced Red Pepper (120 grams or 4 oz)
30 grams or 1 oz of Brazil nuts
200 ml / 7 fl oz of Coconut Milk

Protein 8g, Fat 23g, Carb 20g, Fibre 9g, 331 Kcals

Preparation

Place the nuts or seeds into the Tall Cup. Screw the Nutribullet Extractor Blade on to the top of the cup. Invert the cup, press it down into the Nutribullet Power Base and twist it into place. Blast them for 30 seconds. Put the rest of the solid ingredients into the cup and press them down below the Max Line. Add the fluid base to fill the cup up to the Max Line. Screw the Nutribullet Extractor Blade on to the top of the cup. Invert the cup, press it down into the Nutribullet Power Base and twist it into place. Blast the mixture until it is really smooth (20 or so seconds). *Enjoy!*

Watercress in Rocket

Ingredients

1 Cup/Handful of Watercress (40 grams or 1½ oz)
1 Cup/Handful of Rocket/Arugura Lettuce (40 grams or 1½ oz)
¾ Cup of Avocado slices (90 grams or 3 oz)
1 Cup/Handful of sliced Carrots (120 grams or 4 oz)
200 ml / 7 fl oz of Almond Milk (Unsweetened)

Protein 5g, Fat 16g, Carb 11g, Fibre 11g, 229 Kcals

Preparation

Put all the solid ingredients into the Tall Cup and press them down below the Max Line. Add the fluid base to fill the cup up to the Max Line. Screw the Nutribullet Extractor Blade on to the top of the cup. Invert the cup, press it down into the Nutribullet Power Base and twist it into place. Blast the mixture until it is really smooth (20 or so seconds). **Enjoy!**

Lettuce needs Bok Choy

Ingredients

1 Cup/Handful of Lettuce Leaves (40 grams or 1½ oz)
1 Cup/Handful of Bok Choy (40 grams or 1½ oz)
¾ Cup of Melon chunks (90 grams or 3 oz)
1 Cup/Handful of sliced Green Pepper (120 grams or 4 oz)
200 ml / 7 fl oz of Almond Milk (Unsweetened)

Protein 3g, Fat 3g, Carb 12g, Fibre 5g, 94 Kcals

Preparation

Put all the solid ingredients into the Tall Cup and press them down below the Max Line. Add the fluid base to fill the cup up to the Max Line. Screw the Nutribullet Extractor Blade on to the top of the cup. Invert the cup, press it down into the Nutribullet Power Base and twist it into place. Blast the mixture until it is really smooth (20 or so seconds). **Enjoy!**

Plum Party

Ingredients

2 Cups/Handfuls of Mint (80 grams or 3 oz)
¾ Cup of Plum halves (90 grams or 3 oz)
1 Cup/Handful of sliced Asparagus (120 grams or 4 oz)
200 ml / 7 fl oz of Almond Milk (Unsweetened)

Protein 7g, Fat 3g, Carb 13g, Fibre 10g, 126 Kcals

Preparation

Put all the solid ingredients into the Tall Cup and press them down below the Max Line. Add the fluid base to fill the cup up to the Max Line. Screw the Nutribullet Extractor Blade on to the top of the cup. Invert the cup, press it down into the Nutribullet Power Base and twist it into place. Blast the mixture until it is really smooth (20 or so seconds). **Enjoy!**

Verdant Supermodel

Ingredients

1 Cup/Handful of Broccoli Florets (40 grams or 1½ oz)
1 Cup/Handful of Mint (40 grams or 1½ oz)
¾ Cup of Avocado slices (90 grams or 3 oz)
1 Cup/Handful of sliced Celery (120 grams or 4 oz)
100 ml / 3½ fl oz of Coconut Milk
100 ml / 3½ fl oz of Greek Yoghurt

Protein 9g, Fat 24g, Carb 14g, Fibre 12g, 339 Kcals

Preparation

Put all the solid ingredients into the Tall Cup and press them down below the Max Line. Add the fluid base to fill the cup up to the Max Line. Screw the Nutribullet Extractor Blade on to the top of the cup. Invert the cup, press it down into the Nutribullet Power Base and twist it into place. Blast the mixture until it is really smooth (20 or so seconds). **Enjoy!**

Orange and Red Pepper Chorus

Ingredients

2 Cups/Handfuls of Rocket/Arugura Lettuce (80 grams or 3 oz)
¾ Cup of Orange segments (90 grams or 3 oz)
1 Cup/Handful of sliced Red Pepper (120 grams or 4 oz)
200 ml / 7 fl oz of Almond Milk (Unsweetened)

Protein 4g, Fat 3g, Carb 15g, Fibre 7g, 117 Kcals

Preparation

Put all the solid ingredients into the Tall Cup and press them down below the Max Line. Add the fluid base to fill the cup up to the Max Line. Screw the Nutribullet Extractor Blade on to the top of the cup. Invert the cup, press it down into the Nutribullet Power Base and twist it into place. Blast the mixture until it is really smooth (20 or so seconds). **Enjoy!**

Zucchini Dream

Ingredients

1 Cup/Handful of Mint (40 grams or 1½ oz)
1 Cup/Handful of Broccoli Florets (40 grams or 1½ oz)
¾ Cup of Blackberries (90 grams or 3 oz)
1 Cup/Handful of sliced Zucchini/Courgette (120 grams or 4 oz)
200 ml / 7 fl oz of Hazelnut Milk

Protein 6g, Fat 4g, Carb 15g, Fibre 10g, 148 Kcals

Preparation

Put all the solid ingredients into the Tall Cup and press them down below the Max Line. Add the fluid base to fill the cup up to the Max Line. Screw the Nutribullet Extractor Blade on to the top of the cup. Invert the cup, press it down into the Nutribullet Power Base and twist it into place. Blast the mixture until it is really smooth (20 or so seconds). **Enjoy!**

Rocket and Spinach Power

Ingredients

1 Cup/Handful of Rocket/Arugura Lettuce (40 grams or 1½ oz)
1 Cup/Handful of Spinach (40 grams or 1½ oz)
¾ Cup of Raspberries (90 grams or 3 oz)
1 Cup/Handful of sliced Red Pepper (120 grams or 4 oz)
200 ml / 7 fl oz of Coconut Milk

Protein 4g, Fat 3g, Carb 16g, Fibre 10g, 139 Kcals

Preparation

Put all the solid ingredients into the Tall Cup and press them down below the Max Line. Add the fluid base to fill the cup up to the Max Line. Screw the Nutribullet Extractor Blade on to the top of the cup. Invert the cup, press it down into the Nutribullet Power Base and twist it into place. Blast the mixture until it is really smooth (20 or so seconds). *Enjoy!*

Black Kale goes Melon

Ingredients

1 Cup/Handful of Black Kale de-stemmed (40 grams or 1½ oz)
1 Cup/Handful of Watercress (40 grams or 1½ oz)
¾ Cup of Melon chunks (90 grams or 3 oz)
1 Cup/Handful of sliced Cucumber (120 grams or 4 oz)
200 ml / 7 fl oz of Hazelnut Milk

Protein 4g, Fat 4g, Carb 16g, Fibre 3g, 123 Kcals

Preparation

Put all the solid ingredients into the Tall Cup and press them down below the Max Line. Add the fluid base to fill the cup up to the Max Line. Screw the Nutribullet Extractor Blade on to the top of the cup. Invert the cup, press it down into the Nutribullet Power Base and twist it into place. Blast the mixture until it is really smooth (20 or so seconds). *Enjoy!*

Mint loves Water Melon

Ingredients

1 Cup/Handful of Mint (40 grams or 1½ oz)
1 Cup/Handful of Broccoli Florets (40 grams or 1½ oz)
¾ Cup of Water Melon chunks (90 grams or 3 oz)
1 Cup/Handful of Radishes (120 grams or 4 oz)
100 ml / 3½ fl oz of Almond Milk (Unsweetened)
100 ml / 3½ fl oz of Greek Yoghurt

Protein 8g, Fat 11g, Carb 16g, Fibre 6g, 215 Kcals

Preparation

Put all the solid ingredients into the Tall Cup and press them down below the Max Line. Add the fluid base to fill the cup up to the Max Line. Screw the Nutribullet Extractor Blade on to the top of the cup. Invert the cup, press it down into the Nutribullet Power Base and twist it into place. Blast the mixture until it is really smooth (20 or so seconds). *Enjoy!*

Green Cabbage embraces Strawberry

Ingredients

1 Cup/Handful of Watercress (40 grams or 1½ oz)
1 Cup/Handful of Green Cabbage (40 grams or 1½ oz)
¾ Cup of Strawberries (90 grams or 3 oz)
1 Cup/Handful of sliced Fine Beans (120 grams or 4 oz)
200 ml / 7 fl oz of Hazelnut Milk

Protein 5g, Fat 4g, Carb 17g, Fibre 6g, 131 Kcals

Preparation

Put all the solid ingredients into the Tall Cup and press them down below the Max Line. Add the fluid base to fill the cup up to the Max Line. Screw the Nutribullet Extractor Blade on to the top of the cup. Invert the cup, press it down into the Nutribullet Power Base and twist it into place. Blast the mixture until it is really smooth (20 or so seconds). *Enjoy!*

Pineapple and Fine Bean Crush

Ingredients

1 Cup/Handful of Fennel (40 grams or 1½ oz)
1 Cup/Handful of Lettuce Leaves (40 grams or 1½ oz)
¾ Cup of Pineapple chunks (90 grams or 3 oz)
1 Cup/Handful of sliced Fine Beans (120 grams or 4 oz)
200 ml / 7 fl oz of Almond Milk (Unsweetened)

Protein 5g, Fat 3g, Carb 17g, Fibre 7g, 120 Kcals

Preparation

Put all the solid ingredients into the Tall Cup and press them down below the Max Line. Add the fluid base to fill the cup up to the Max Line. Screw the Nutribullet Extractor Blade on to the top of the cup. Invert the cup, press it down into the Nutribullet Power Base and twist it into place. Blast the mixture until it is really smooth (20 or so seconds). **Enjoy!**

Green Cabbage on Apricot

Ingredients

1 Cup/Handful of Spinach (40 grams or 1½ oz)
1 Cup/Handful of Green Cabbage (40 grams or 1½ oz)
¾ Cup of Apricot halves (90 grams or 3 oz)
1 Cup/Handful of sliced Asparagus (120 grams or 4 oz)
200 ml / 7 fl oz of Coconut Milk

Protein 6g, Fat 2g, Carb 18g, Fibre 6g, 126 Kcals

Preparation

Put all the solid ingredients into the Tall Cup and press them down below the Max Line. Add the fluid base to fill the cup up to the Max Line. Screw the Nutribullet Extractor Blade on to the top of the cup. Invert the cup, press it down into the Nutribullet Power Base and twist it into place. Blast the mixture until it is really smooth (20 or so seconds). **Enjoy!**

Bok Choy needs Nectarine

Ingredients

1 Cup/Handful of Bok Choy (40 grams or 1½ oz)
1 Cup/Handful of Watercress (40 grams or 1½ oz)
¾ Cup of Nectarine segments (90 grams or 3 oz)
1 Cup/Handful of sliced Cauliflower florets (120 grams or 4 oz)
100 ml / 3½ fl oz of Almond Milk (Unsweetened)
100 ml / 3½ fl oz of Greek Yoghurt

Protein 9g, Fat 11g, Carb 18g, Fibre 5g, 217 Kcals

Preparation

Put all the solid ingredients into the Tall Cup and press them down below the Max Line. Add the fluid base to fill the cup up to the Max Line. Screw the Nutribullet Extractor Blade on to the top of the cup. Invert the cup, press it down into the Nutribullet Power Base and twist it into place. Blast the mixture until it is really smooth (20 or so seconds). *Enjoy!*

Cranberry on Celery

Ingredients

2 Cups/Handfuls of Black Kale de-stemmed (80 grams or 3 oz)
¾ Cup of Cranberries (90 grams or 3 oz)
1 Cup/Handful of sliced Celery (120 grams or 4 oz)
100 ml / 3½ fl oz of Hazelnut Milk
100 ml / 3½ fl oz of Greek Yoghurt

Protein 8g, Fat 13g, Carb 18g, Fibre 8g, 242 Kcals

Preparation

Put all the solid ingredients into the Tall Cup and press them down below the Max Line. Add the fluid base to fill the cup up to the Max Line. Screw the Nutribullet Extractor Blade on to the top of the cup. Invert the cup, press it down into the Nutribullet Power Base and twist it into place. Blast the mixture until it is really smooth (20 or so seconds). *Enjoy!*

Mint and Peach Breeze

Ingredients

1 Cup/Handful of Bok Choy (40 grams or 1½ oz)
1 Cup/Handful of Mint (40 grams or 1½ oz)
¾ Cup of Peach slices (90 grams or 3 oz)
1 Cup/Handful of sliced Red Pepper (120 grams or 4 oz)
200 ml / 7 fl oz of Coconut Milk

Protein 4g, Fat 3g, Carb 18g, Fibre 7g, 135 Kcals

Preparation

Put all the solid ingredients into the Tall Cup and press them down below the Max Line. Add the fluid base to fill the cup up to the Max Line. Screw the Nutribullet Extractor Blade on to the top of the cup. Invert the cup, press it down into the Nutribullet Power Base and twist it into place. Blast the mixture until it is really smooth (20 or so seconds). **Enjoy!**

Tangerine Tango

Ingredients

2 Cups/Handfuls of Lettuce Leaves (80 grams or 3 oz)
¾ Cup of Tangerine slices (90 grams or 3 oz)
1 Cup/Handful of sliced Cucumber (120 grams or 4 oz)
100 ml / 3½ fl oz of Almond Milk (Unsweetened)
100 ml / 3½ fl oz of Greek Yoghurt

Protein 7g, Fat 11g, Carb 19g, Fibre 5g, 213 Kcals

Preparation

Put all the solid ingredients into the Tall Cup and press them down below the Max Line. Add the fluid base to fill the cup up to the Max Line. Screw the Nutribullet Extractor Blade on to the top of the cup. Invert the cup, press it down into the Nutribullet Power Base and twist it into place. Blast the mixture until it is really smooth (20 or so seconds). **Enjoy!**

Water Melon Waterfall

Ingredients

1 Cup/Handful of Green Cabbage (40 grams or 1½ oz)
1 Cup/Handful of Bok Choy (40 grams or 1½ oz)
¾ Cup of Water Melon chunks (90 grams or 3 oz)
1 Cup/Handful of sliced Cucumber (120 grams or 4 oz)
200 ml / 7 fl oz of Dairy Milk Whole

Protein 9g, Fat 8g, Carb 19g, Fibre 3g, 184 Kcals

Preparation

Put all the solid ingredients into the Tall Cup and press them down below the Max Line. Add the fluid base to fill the cup up to the Max Line. Screw the Nutribullet Extractor Blade on to the top of the cup. Invert the cup, press it down into the Nutribullet Power Base and twist it into place. Blast the mixture until it is really smooth (20 or so seconds). **Enjoy!**

Fennel and Cranberry Garden

Ingredients

1 Cup/Handful of Spinach (40 grams or 1½ oz)
1 Cup/Handful of Fennel (40 grams or 1½ oz)
¾ Cup of Cranberries (90 grams or 3 oz)
1 Cup/Handful of Radishes (120 grams or 4 oz)
100 ml / 3½ fl oz of Coconut Milk
100 ml / 3½ fl oz of Greek Yoghurt

Protein 7g, Fat 11g, Carb 19g, Fibre 8g, 227 Kcals

Preparation

Put all the solid ingredients into the Tall Cup and press them down below the Max Line. Add the fluid base to fill the cup up to the Max Line. Screw the Nutribullet Extractor Blade on to the top of the cup. Invert the cup, press it down into the Nutribullet Power Base and twist it into place. Blast the mixture until it is really smooth (20 or so seconds). **Enjoy!**

Rocket and Broccoli Blockbuster

Ingredients

1 Cup/Handful of Rocket/Arugura Lettuce (40 grams or 1½ oz)
1 Cup/Handful of Broccoli Florets (40 grams or 1½ oz)
¾ Cup of Plum halves (90 grams or 3 oz)
1 Cup/Handful of diced Beetroot (120 grams or 4 oz)
200 ml / 7 fl oz of Almond Milk (Unsweetened)

Protein 5g, Fat 3g, Carb 20g, Fibre 7g, 138 Kcals

Preparation

Put all the solid ingredients into the Tall Cup and press them down below the Max Line. Add the fluid base to fill the cup up to the Max Line. Screw the Nutribullet Extractor Blade on to the top of the cup. Invert the cup, press it down into the Nutribullet Power Base and twist it into place. Blast the mixture until it is really smooth (20 or so seconds). **Enjoy!**

Strawberry and Green Pepper Explosion

Ingredients

1 Cup/Handful of Spinach (40 grams or 1½ oz)
1 Cup/Handful of Green Cabbage (40 grams or 1½ oz)
¾ Cup of Strawberries (90 grams or 3 oz)
1 Cup/Handful of sliced Green Pepper (120 grams or 4 oz)
200 ml / 7 fl oz of Dairy Milk Whole

Protein 10g, Fat 8g, Carb 20g, Fibre 6g, 200 Kcals

Preparation

Put all the solid ingredients into the Tall Cup and press them down below the Max Line. Add the fluid base to fill the cup up to the Max Line. Screw the Nutribullet Extractor Blade on to the top of the cup. Invert the cup, press it down into the Nutribullet Power Base and twist it into place. Blast the mixture until it is really smooth (20 or so seconds). **Enjoy!**

Classic Low Carb Blasts with Flavour Boosts - *All less than 20 Carb grams*

Mint and Strawberry Miracle

Ingredients

1 Cup/Handful of Broccoli Florets (40 grams or 1½ oz)
1 Cup/Handful of Mint (40 grams or 1½ oz)
¾ Cup of Strawberries (90 grams or 3 oz)
1 Cup/Handful of sliced Cauliflower florets (120 grams or 4 oz)
30 grams or 1 oz of Pecans
200 ml / 7 fl oz of Almond Milk (Unsweetened)
25 grams or 7/8 oz of Pea Protein
Protein 28g, Fat 26g, Carb 15g, Fibre 12g, 425 Kcals

Preparation

Place the nuts or seeds into the Tall Cup. Screw the Nutribullet Extractor Blade on to the top of the cup. Invert the cup, press it down into the Nutribullet Power Base and twist it into place. Blast them for 30 seconds. Put the rest of the solid ingredients into the cup and press them down below the Max Line. Add the fluid base to fill the cup up to the Max Line. Screw the Nutribullet Extractor Blade on to the top of the cup. Invert the cup, press it down into the Nutribullet Power Base and twist it into place. Blast the mixture until it is really smooth (20 or so seconds). *Enjoy!*

Watercress embraces Ginger Root

Ingredients

1 Cup/Handful of Watercress (40 grams or 1½ oz)
1 Cup/Handful of Bok Choy (40 grams or 1½ oz)
¾ Cup of Water Melon chunks (90 grams or 3 oz)
1 Cup/Handful of sliced Red Pepper (120 grams or 4 oz)
22 grams or ¾ oz of Flax Seeds
200 ml / 7 fl oz of Almond Milk (Unsweetened)
22 grams or ¾ oz of Ginger Root
Protein 8g, Fat 12g, Carb 16g, Fibre 11g, 234 Kcals

Preparation

Place the nuts or seeds into the Tall Cup. Screw the Nutribullet Extractor Blade on to the top of the cup. Invert the cup, press it down into the Nutribullet Power Base and twist it into place. Blast them for 30 seconds. Put the rest of the solid ingredients into the cup and press them down below the Max Line. Add the fluid base to fill the cup up to the Max Line. Screw the Nutribullet Extractor Blade on to the top of the cup. Invert the cup, press it down into the Nutribullet Power Base and twist it into place. Blast the mixture until it is really smooth (20 or so seconds). *Enjoy!*

Sunflower Splash

Ingredients

1 Cup/Handful of Rocket/Arugura Lettuce (40 grams or 1½ oz)
1 Cup/Handful of Watercress (40 grams or 1½ oz)
¾ Cup of Strawberries (90 grams or 3 oz)
1 Cup/Handful of sliced Red Pepper (120 grams or 4 oz)
22 grams or ¾ oz of Sunflower Seeds Hulled
200 ml / 7 fl oz of Almond Milk (Unsweetened)
25 grams or 7/8 oz of Rice Protein

Protein 28g, Fat 14g, Carb 16g, Fibre 7g, 309 Kcals

Preparation

Place the nuts or seeds into the Tall Cup. Screw the Nutribullet Extractor Blade on to the top of the cup. Invert the cup, press it down into the Nutribullet Power Base and twist it into place. Blast them for 30 seconds. Put the rest of the solid ingredients into the cup and press them down below the Max Line. Add the fluid base to fill the cup up to the Max Line. Screw the Nutribullet Extractor Blade on to the top of the cup. Invert the cup, press it down into the Nutribullet Power Base and twist it into place. Blast the mixture until it is really smooth (20 or so seconds). ***Enjoy!***

Plum and Tomato Morning

Ingredients

1 Cup/Handful of Rocket/Arugura Lettuce (40 grams or 1½ oz)
1 Cup/Handful of Spinach (40 grams or 1½ oz)
¾ Cup of Plum halves (90 grams or 3 oz)
1 Cup/Handful of sliced Tomato (120 grams or 4 oz)
22 grams or ¾ oz of Flax Seeds
200 ml / 7 fl oz of Almond Milk (Unsweetened)
25 grams or 7/8 oz of Pea Protein

Protein 28g, Fat 13g, Carb 17g, Fibre 11g, 323 Kcals

Preparation

Place the nuts or seeds into the Tall Cup. Screw the Nutribullet Extractor Blade on to the top of the cup. Invert the cup, press it down into the Nutribullet Power Base and twist it into place. Blast them for 30 seconds. Put the rest of the solid ingredients into the cup and press them down below the Max Line. Add the fluid base to fill the cup up to the Max Line. Screw the Nutribullet Extractor Blade on to the top of the cup. Invert the cup, press it down into the Nutribullet Power Base and twist it into place. Blast the mixture until it is really smooth (20 or so seconds). ***Enjoy!***

Apricot and Cucumber Mist

Ingredients

1 Cup/Handful of Bok Choy (40 grams or 1½ oz)
1 Cup/Handful of Green Cabbage (40 grams or 1½ oz)
¾ Cup of Apricot halves (90 grams or 3 oz)
1 Cup/Handful of sliced Cucumber (120 grams or 4 oz)
22 grams or ¾ oz of Pumpkin Seeds
200 ml / 7 fl oz of Almond Milk (Unsweetened)
25 grams or 7/8 oz of Pea Protein

Protein 29g, Fat 13g, Carb 17g, Fibre 6g, 324 Kcals

Preparation

Place the nuts or seeds into the Tall Cup. Screw the Nutribullet Extractor Blade on to the top of the cup. Invert the cup, press it down into the Nutribullet Power Base and twist it into place. Blast them for 30 seconds. Put the rest of the solid ingredients into the cup and press them down below the Max Line. Add the fluid base to fill the cup up to the Max Line. Screw the Nutribullet Extractor Blade on to the top of the cup. Invert the cup, press it down into the Nutribullet Power Base and twist it into place. Blast the mixture until it is really smooth (20 or so seconds). **Enjoy!**

Chlorella Consortium

Ingredients

1 Cup/Handful of Green Cabbage (40 grams or 1½ oz)
1 Cup/Handful of Red or White Cabbage (40 grams or 1½ oz)
¾ Cup of Peach slices (90 grams or 3 oz)
1 Cup/Handful of sliced Cucumber (120 grams or 4 oz)
30 grams or 1 oz of Peanuts
200 ml / 7 fl oz of Almond Milk (Unsweetened)
15 grams or ½ oz of Chlorella

Protein 19g, Fat 19g, Carb 17g, Fibre 7g, 321 Kcals

Preparation

Place the nuts or seeds into the Tall Cup. Screw the Nutribullet Extractor Blade on to the top of the cup. Invert the cup, press it down into the Nutribullet Power Base and twist it into place. Blast them for 30 seconds. Put the rest of the solid ingredients into the cup and press them down below the Max Line. Add the fluid base to fill the cup up to the Max Line. Screw the Nutribullet Extractor Blade on to the top of the cup. Invert the cup, press it down into the Nutribullet Power Base and twist it into place. Blast the mixture until it is really smooth (20 or so seconds). **Enjoy!**

Fruity Splendour

Ingredients

2 Cups/Handfuls of Rocket/Arugura Lettuce (80 grams or 3 oz)
¾ Cup of Strawberries (90 grams or 3 oz)
1 Cup/Handful of sliced Celery (120 grams or 4 oz)
30 grams or 1 oz of Peanuts
200 ml / 7 fl oz of Hazelnut Milk
25 grams or 7/8 oz of Whey Protein (unflavoured)

Protein 31g, Fat 20g, Carb 18g, Fibre 8g, 388 Kcals

Preparation

Place the nuts or seeds into the Tall Cup. Screw the Nutribullet Extractor Blade on to the top of the cup. Invert the cup, press it down into the Nutribullet Power Base and twist it into place. Blast them for 30 seconds. Put the rest of the solid ingredients into the cup and press them down below the Max Line. Add the fluid base to fill the cup up to the Max Line. Screw the Nutribullet Extractor Blade on to the top of the cup. Invert the cup, press it down into the Nutribullet Power Base and twist it into place. Blast the mixture until it is really smooth (20 or so seconds). **Enjoy!**

Broccoli loves Flax

Ingredients

1 Cup/Handful of Broccoli Florets (40 grams or 1½ oz)
1 Cup/Handful of Green Cabbage (40 grams or 1½ oz)
¾ Cup of Blackberries (90 grams or 3 oz)
1 Cup/Handful of sliced Fine Beans (120 grams or 4 oz)
22 grams or ¾ oz of Flax Seeds
200 ml / 7 fl oz of Coconut Milk
25 grams or 7/8 oz of Whey Protein (unflavoured)

Protein 29g, Fat 14g, Carb 18g, Fibre 15g, 350 Kcals

Preparation

Place the nuts or seeds into the Tall Cup. Screw the Nutribullet Extractor Blade on to the top of the cup. Invert the cup, press it down into the Nutribullet Power Base and twist it into place. Blast them for 30 seconds. Put the rest of the solid ingredients into the cup and press them down below the Max Line. Add the fluid base to fill the cup up to the Max Line. Screw the Nutribullet Extractor Blade on to the top of the cup. Invert the cup, press it down into the Nutribullet Power Base and twist it into place. Blast the mixture until it is really smooth (20 or so seconds). **Enjoy!**

Green Pepper loves Cocoa Chocolate

Ingredients

1 Cup/Handful of Lettuce Leaves (40 grams or 1½ oz)
1 Cup/Handful of Spinach (40 grams or 1½ oz)
¾ Cup of Avocado slices (90 grams or 3 oz)
1 Cup/Handful of sliced Green Pepper (120 grams or 4 oz)
30 grams or 1 oz of Pecans
200 ml / 7 fl oz of Hazelnut Milk
22 grams or ¾ oz of 85% Cocoa Chocolate

Protein 10g, Fat 49g, Carb 18g, Fibre 17g, 577 Kcals

Preparation

Place the nuts or seeds into the Tall Cup. Screw the Nutribullet Extractor Blade on to the top of the cup. Invert the cup, press it down into the Nutribullet Power Base and twist it into place. Blast them for 30 seconds. Put the rest of the solid ingredients into the cup and press them down below the Max Line. Add the fluid base to fill the cup up to the Max Line. Screw the Nutribullet Extractor Blade on to the top of the cup. Invert the cup, press it down into the Nutribullet Power Base and twist it into place. Blast the mixture until it is really smooth (20 or so seconds). **Enjoy!**

Mint and Flax Blizzard

Ingredients

1 Cup/Handful of Black Kale de-stemmed (40 grams or 1½ oz)
1 Cup/Handful of Mint (40 grams or 1½ oz)
¾ Cup of Tangerine slices (90 grams or 3 oz)
1 Cup/Handful of sliced Tomato (120 grams or 4 oz)
22 grams or ¾ oz of Flax Seeds
200 ml / 7 fl oz of Almond Milk (Unsweetened)
25 grams or 7/8 oz of Rice Protein

Protein 29g, Fat 13g, Carb 18g, Fibre 14g, 337 Kcals

Preparation

Place the nuts or seeds into the Tall Cup. Screw the Nutribullet Extractor Blade on to the top of the cup. Invert the cup, press it down into the Nutribullet Power Base and twist it into place. Blast them for 30 seconds. Put the rest of the solid ingredients into the cup and press them down below the Max Line. Add the fluid base to fill the cup up to the Max Line. Screw the Nutribullet Extractor Blade on to the top of the cup. Invert the cup, press it down into the Nutribullet Power Base and twist it into place. Blast the mixture until it is really smooth (20 or so seconds). **Enjoy!**

Kiwi Kiss

Ingredients

2 Cups/Handfuls of Spinach (80 grams or 3 oz)
¾ Cup of Kiwi Fruit slices (90 grams or 3 oz)
1 Cup/Handful of sliced Celery (120 grams or 4 oz)
30 grams or 1 oz of Walnuts
200 ml / 7 fl oz of Almond Milk (Unsweetened)
25 grams or 7/8 oz of Rice Protein

Protein 30g, Fat 23g, Carb 18g, Fibre 9g, 407 Kcals

Preparation

Place the nuts or seeds into the Tall Cup. Screw the Nutribullet Extractor Blade on to the top of the cup. Invert the cup, press it down into the Nutribullet Power Base and twist it into place. Blast them for 30 seconds. Put the rest of the solid ingredients into the cup and press them down below the Max Line. Add the fluid base to fill the cup up to the Max Line. Screw the Nutribullet Extractor Blade on to the top of the cup. Invert the cup, press it down into the Nutribullet Power Base and twist it into place. Blast the mixture until it is really smooth (20 or so seconds). ***Enjoy!***

Watercress and Chlorella Vision

Ingredients

1 Cup/Handful of Watercress (40 grams or 1½ oz)
1 Cup/Handful of Broccoli Florets (40 grams or 1½ oz)
¾ Cup of Blackberries (90 grams or 3 oz)
1 Cup/Handful of Radishes (120 grams or 4 oz)
30 grams or 1 oz of Walnuts
100 ml / 3½ fl oz of Almond Milk (Unsweetened)
100 ml / 3½ fl oz of Greek Yoghurt
15 grams or ½ oz of Chlorella

Protein 21g, Fat 32g, Carb 18g, Fibre 10g, 463 Kcals

Preparation

Place the nuts or seeds into the Tall Cup. Screw the Nutribullet Extractor Blade on to the top of the cup. Invert the cup, press it down into the Nutribullet Power Base and twist it into place. Blast them for 30 seconds. Put the rest of the solid ingredients into the cup and press them down below the Max Line. Add the fluid base to fill the cup up to the Max Line. Screw the Nutribullet Extractor Blade on to the top of the cup. Invert the cup, press it down into the Nutribullet Power Base and twist it into place. Blast the mixture until it is really smooth (20 or so seconds). ***Enjoy!***

Swede and Spirulina Boost

Ingredients

1 Cup/Handful of Broccoli Florets (40 grams or 1½ oz)
1 Cup/Handful of Fennel (40 grams or 1½ oz)
¾ Cup of Raspberries (90 grams or 3 oz)
1 Cup/Handful of diced Swede (120 grams or 4 oz)
22 grams or ¾ oz of Flax Seeds
200 ml / 7 fl oz of Almond Milk (Unsweetened)
15 grams or ½ oz of Spirulina

Protein 17g, Fat 14g, Carb 18g, Fibre 17g, 293 Kcals

Preparation

Place the nuts or seeds into the Tall Cup. Screw the Nutribullet Extractor Blade on to the top of the cup. Invert the cup, press it down into the Nutribullet Power Base and twist it into place. Blast them for 30 seconds. Put the rest of the solid ingredients into the cup and press them down below the Max Line. Add the fluid base to fill the cup up to the Max Line. Screw the Nutribullet Extractor Blade on to the top of the cup. Invert the cup, press it down into the Nutribullet Power Base and twist it into place. Blast the mixture until it is really smooth (20 or so seconds). **Enjoy!**

Watercress and Ginger Root Sonata

Ingredients

2 Cups/Handfuls of Watercress (80 grams or 3 oz)
¾ Cup of Avocado slices (90 grams or 3 oz)
1 Cup/Handful of sliced Green Pepper (120 grams or 4 oz)
30 grams or 1 oz of Brazil nuts
100 ml / 3½ fl oz of Coconut Milk
100 ml / 3½ fl oz of Greek Yoghurt
22 grams or ¾ oz of Ginger Root

Protein 14g, Fat 44g, Carb 19g, Fibre 11g, 537 Kcals

Preparation

Place the nuts or seeds into the Tall Cup. Screw the Nutribullet Extractor Blade on to the top of the cup. Invert the cup, press it down into the Nutribullet Power Base and twist it into place. Blast them for 30 seconds. Put the rest of the solid ingredients into the cup and press them down below the Max Line. Add the fluid base to fill the cup up to the Max Line. Screw the Nutribullet Extractor Blade on to the top of the cup. Invert the cup, press it down into the Nutribullet Power Base and twist it into place. Blast the mixture until it is really smooth (20 or so seconds). **Enjoy!**

Raspberry and Chlorella Dictator

Ingredients

1 Cup/Handful of Rocket/Arugura Lettuce (40 grams or 1½ oz)
1 Cup/Handful of Lettuce Leaves (40 grams or 1½ oz)
¾ Cup of Raspberries (90 grams or 3 oz)
1 Cup/Handful of sliced Cauliflower florets (120 grams or 4 oz)
30 grams or 1 oz of Pecans
200 ml / 7 fl oz of Coconut Milk
15 grams or ½ oz of Chlorella

Protein 15g, Fat 26g, Carb 19g, Fibre 12g, 390 Kcals

Preparation

Place the nuts or seeds into the Tall Cup. Screw the Nutribullet Extractor Blade on to the top of the cup. Invert the cup, press it down into the Nutribullet Power Base and twist it into place. Blast them for 30 seconds. Put the rest of the solid ingredients into the cup and press them down below the Max Line. Add the fluid base to fill the cup up to the Max Line. Screw the Nutribullet Extractor Blade on to the top of the cup. Invert the cup, press it down into the Nutribullet Power Base and twist it into place. Blast the mixture until it is really smooth (20 or so seconds). ***Enjoy!***

Mint in Tangerine

Ingredients

1 Cup/Handful of Spinach (40 grams or 1½ oz)
1 Cup/Handful of Mint (40 grams or 1½ oz)
¾ Cup of Tangerine slices (90 grams or 3 oz)
1 Cup/Handful of sliced Cauliflower florets (120 grams or 4 oz)
30 grams or 1 oz of Brazil nuts
200 ml / 7 fl oz of Almond Milk (Unsweetened)
15 grams or ½ oz of Chlorella

Protein 18g, Fat 25g, Carb 19g, Fibre 11g, 381 Kcals

Preparation

Place the nuts or seeds into the Tall Cup. Screw the Nutribullet Extractor Blade on to the top of the cup. Invert the cup, press it down into the Nutribullet Power Base and twist it into place. Blast them for 30 seconds. Put the rest of the solid ingredients into the cup and press them down below the Max Line. Add the fluid base to fill the cup up to the Max Line. Screw the Nutribullet Extractor Blade on to the top of the cup. Invert the cup, press it down into the Nutribullet Power Base and twist it into place. Blast the mixture until it is really smooth (20 or so seconds). ***Enjoy!***

Red Cabbage Rush

Ingredients

1 Cup/Handful of Red or White Cabbage (40 grams or 1½ oz)
1 Cup/Handful of Mint (40 grams or 1½ oz)
¾ Cup of Clementine slices (90 grams or 3 oz)
1 Cup/Handful of sliced Zucchini/Courgette (120 grams or 4 oz)
30 grams or 1 oz of Brazil nuts
200 ml / 7 fl oz of Almond Milk (Unsweetened)
22 grams or ¾ oz of Ginger Root

Protein 10g, Fat 23g, Carb 20g, Fibre 10g, 333 Kcals

Preparation

Place the nuts or seeds into the Tall Cup. Screw the Nutribullet Extractor Blade on to the top of the cup. Invert the cup, press it down into the Nutribullet Power Base and twist it into place. Blast them for 30 seconds. Put the rest of the solid ingredients into the cup and press them down below the Max Line. Add the fluid base to fill the cup up to the Max Line. Screw the Nutribullet Extractor Blade on to the top of the cup. Invert the cup, press it down into the Nutribullet Power Base and twist it into place. Blast the mixture until it is really smooth (20 or so seconds). *Enjoy!*

Lettuce and Almond Revision

Ingredients

1 Cup/Handful of Lettuce Leaves (40 grams or 1½ oz)
1 Cup/Handful of Black Kale de-stemmed (40 grams or 1½ oz)
¾ Cup of Strawberries (90 grams or 3 oz)
1 Cup/Handful of Radishes (120 grams or 4 oz)
30 grams or 1 oz of Almonds
100 ml / 3½ fl oz of Almond Milk (Unsweetened)
100 ml / 3½ fl oz of Greek Yoghurt
22 grams or ¾ oz of Ginger Root

Protein 15g, Fat 28g, Carb 20g, Fibre 9g, 401 Kcals

Preparation

Place the nuts or seeds into the Tall Cup. Screw the Nutribullet Extractor Blade on to the top of the cup. Invert the cup, press it down into the Nutribullet Power Base and twist it into place. Blast them for 30 seconds. Put the rest of the solid ingredients into the cup and press them down below the Max Line. Add the fluid base to fill the cup up to the Max Line. Screw the Nutribullet Extractor Blade on to the top of the cup. Invert the cup, press it down into the Nutribullet Power Base and twist it into place. Blast the mixture until it is really smooth (20 or so seconds). *Enjoy!*

Orange and Tomato Presented

Ingredients

1 Cup/Handful of Green Cabbage (40 grams or 1½ oz)
1 Cup/Handful of Broccoli Florets (40 grams or 1½ oz)
¾ Cup of Orange segments (90 grams or 3 oz)
1 Cup/Handful of sliced Tomato (120 grams or 4 oz)
30 grams or 1 oz of Hazelnuts
200 ml / 7 fl oz of Almond Milk (Unsweetened)
25 grams or 7/8 oz of Pea Protein

Protein 28g, Fat 22g, Carb 20g, Fibre 9g, 403 Kcals

Preparation

Place the nuts or seeds into the Tall Cup. Screw the Nutribullet Extractor Blade on to the top of the cup. Invert the cup, press it down into the Nutribullet Power Base and twist it into place. Blast them for 30 seconds. Put the rest of the solid ingredients into the cup and press them down below the Max Line. Add the fluid base to fill the cup up to the Max Line. Screw the Nutribullet Extractor Blade on to the top of the cup. Invert the cup, press it down into the Nutribullet Power Base and twist it into place. Blast the mixture until it is really smooth (20 or so seconds). **Enjoy!**

Zucchini embraces Spirulina

Ingredients

2 Cups/Handfuls of Black Kale de-stemmed (80 grams or 3 oz)
¾ Cup of Avocado slices (90 grams or 3 oz)
1 Cup/Handful of sliced Zucchini/Courgette (120 grams or 4 oz)
22 grams or ¾ oz of Sesame Seeds Hulled
100 ml / 3½ fl oz of Dairy Milk Whole
100 ml / 3½ fl oz of Half Fat Crème Fraiche
15 grams or ½ oz of Spirulina

Protein 22g, Fat 47g, Carb 20g, Fibre 11g, 598 Kcals

Preparation

Place the nuts or seeds into the Tall Cup. Screw the Nutribullet Extractor Blade on to the top of the cup. Invert the cup, press it down into the Nutribullet Power Base and twist it into place. Blast them for 30 seconds. Put the rest of the solid ingredients into the cup and press them down below the Max Line. Add the fluid base to fill the cup up to the Max Line. Screw the Nutribullet Extractor Blade on to the top of the cup. Invert the cup, press it down into the Nutribullet Power Base and twist it into place. Blast the mixture until it is really smooth (20 or so seconds). **Enjoy!**

Fruity Panache

Ingredients

1 Cup/Handful of Lettuce Leaves (40 grams or 1½ oz)
1 Cup/Handful of Rocket/Arugura Lettuce (40 grams or 1½ oz)
¾ Cup of Avocado slices (90 grams or 3 oz)
1 Cup/Handful of sliced Celery (120 grams or 4 oz)
100 ml / 3½ fl oz of Almond Milk (Unsweetened)
100 ml / 3½ fl oz of Greek Yoghurt
25 grams or 7/8 oz of Rice Protein

Protein 28g, Fat 24g, Carb 12g, Fibre 10g, 407 Kcals

Preparation

Put all the solid ingredients into the Tall Cup and press them down below the Max Line. Add the fluid base to fill the cup up to the Max Line. Screw the Nutribullet Extractor Blade on to the top of the cup. Invert the cup, press it down into the Nutribullet Power Base and twist it into place. Blast the mixture until it is really smooth (20 or so seconds). **Enjoy!**

Fennel and Lettuce Utopia

Ingredients

1 Cup/Handful of Fennel (40 grams or 1½ oz)
1 Cup/Handful of Lettuce Leaves (40 grams or 1½ oz)
¾ Cup of Raspberries (90 grams or 3 oz)
1 Cup/Handful of sliced Tomato (120 grams or 4 oz)
200 ml / 7 fl oz of Almond Milk (Unsweetened)
25 grams or 7/8 oz of Whey Protein (flavoured)

Protein 23g, Fat 5g, Carb 13g, Fibre 10g, 222 Kcals

Preparation

Put all the solid ingredients into the Tall Cup and press them down below the Max Line. Add the fluid base to fill the cup up to the Max Line. Screw the Nutribullet Extractor Blade on to the top of the cup. Invert the cup, press it down into the Nutribullet Power Base and twist it into place. Blast the mixture until it is really smooth (20 or so seconds). **Enjoy!**

Raspberry and Spirulina Debut

Ingredients

1 Cup/Handful of Red or White Cabbage (40 grams or 1½ oz)
1 Cup/Handful of Mint (40 grams or 1½ oz)
¾ Cup of Raspberries (90 grams or 3 oz)
1 Cup/Handful of sliced Celery (120 grams or 4 oz)
200 ml / 7 fl oz of Almond Milk (Unsweetened)
15 grams or ½ oz of Spirulina

Protein 13g, Fat 4g, Carb 13g, Fibre 12g, 164 Kcals

Preparation

Put all the solid ingredients into the Tall Cup and press them down below the Max Line. Add the fluid base to fill the cup up to the Max Line. Screw the Nutribullet Extractor Blade on to the top of the cup. Invert the cup, press it down into the Nutribullet Power Base and twist it into place. Blast the mixture until it is really smooth (20 or so seconds). **Enjoy!**

Peach Piazza

Ingredients

1 Cup/Handful of Black Kale de-stemmed (40 grams or 1½ oz)
1 Cup/Handful of Spinach (40 grams or 1½ oz)
¾ Cup of Peach slices (90 grams or 3 oz)
1 Cup/Handful of sliced Cauliflower florets (120 grams or 4 oz)
200 ml / 7 fl oz of Almond Milk (Unsweetened)
25 grams or 7/8 oz of Whey Protein (unflavoured)

Protein 26g, Fat 5g, Carb 14g, Fibre 6g, 214 Kcals

Preparation

Put all the solid ingredients into the Tall Cup and press them down below the Max Line. Add the fluid base to fill the cup up to the Max Line. Screw the Nutribullet Extractor Blade on to the top of the cup. Invert the cup, press it down into the Nutribullet Power Base and twist it into place. Blast the mixture until it is really smooth (20 or so seconds). **Enjoy!**

Grapefruit and Cucumber Guru

Ingredients

1 Cup/Handful of Spinach (40 grams or 1½ oz)
1 Cup/Handful of Black Kale de-stemmed (40 grams or 1½ oz)
¾ Cup of Grapefruit segments (90 grams or 3 oz)
1 Cup/Handful of sliced Cucumber (120 grams or 4 oz)
200 ml / 7 fl oz of Almond Milk (Unsweetened)
22 grams or ¾ oz of 85% Cocoa Chocolate

Protein 7g, Fat 14g, Carb 14g, Fibre 8g, 221 Kcals

Preparation

Put all the solid ingredients into the Tall Cup and press them down below the Max Line. Add the fluid base to fill the cup up to the Max Line. Screw the Nutribullet Extractor Blade on to the top of the cup. Invert the cup, press it down into the Nutribullet Power Base and twist it into place. Blast the mixture until it is really smooth (20 or so seconds). **Enjoy!**

Watercress and Black Kale Treat

Ingredients

1 Cup/Handful of Watercress (40 grams or 1½ oz)
1 Cup/Handful of Black Kale de-stemmed (40 grams or 1½ oz)
¾ Cup of Avocado slices (90 grams or 3 oz)
1 Cup/Handful of sliced Asparagus (120 grams or 4 oz)
100 ml / 3½ fl oz of Coconut Milk
100 ml / 3½ fl oz of Greek Yoghurt
25 grams or 7/8 oz of Whey Protein (flavoured)

Protein 30g, Fat 26g, Carb 15g, Fibre 10g, 440 Kcals

Preparation

Put all the solid ingredients into the Tall Cup and press them down below the Max Line. Add the fluid base to fill the cup up to the Max Line. Screw the Nutribullet Extractor Blade on to the top of the cup. Invert the cup, press it down into the Nutribullet Power Base and twist it into place. Blast the mixture until it is really smooth (20 or so seconds). **Enjoy!**

Green Cabbage and Raspberry Delivered

Ingredients

1 Cup/Handful of Green Cabbage (40 grams or 1½ oz)
1 Cup/Handful of Lettuce Leaves (40 grams or 1½ oz)
¾ Cup of Raspberries (90 grams or 3 oz)
1 Cup/Handful of sliced Asparagus (120 grams or 4 oz)
200 ml / 7 fl oz of Coconut Milk
25 grams or 7/8 oz of Whey Protein (unflavoured)

Protein 25g, Fat 4g, Carb 16g, Fibre 10g, 228 Kcals

Preparation

Put all the solid ingredients into the Tall Cup and press them down below the Max Line. Add the fluid base to fill the cup up to the Max Line. Screw the Nutribullet Extractor Blade on to the top of the cup. Invert the cup, press it down into the Nutribullet Power Base and twist it into place. Blast the mixture until it is really smooth (20 or so seconds). **Enjoy!**

Water Melon goes Tomato

Ingredients

2 Cups/Handfuls of Broccoli Florets (80 grams or 3 oz)
¾ Cup of Water Melon chunks (90 grams or 3 oz)
1 Cup/Handful of sliced Tomato (120 grams or 4 oz)
200 ml / 7 fl oz of Almond Milk (Unsweetened)
25 grams or 7/8 oz of Pea Protein

Protein 24g, Fat 4g, Carb 16g, Fibre 5g, 203 Kcals

Preparation

Put all the solid ingredients into the Tall Cup and press them down below the Max Line. Add the fluid base to fill the cup up to the Max Line. Screw the Nutribullet Extractor Blade on to the top of the cup. Invert the cup, press it down into the Nutribullet Power Base and twist it into place. Blast the mixture until it is really smooth (20 or so seconds). **Enjoy!**

Orange needs Tomato

Ingredients

2 Cups/Handfuls of Mint (80 grams or 3 oz)
¾ Cup of Orange segments (90 grams or 3 oz)
1 Cup/Handful of sliced Tomato (120 grams or 4 oz)
200 ml / 7 fl oz of Almond Milk (Unsweetened)
25 grams or 7/8 oz of Pea Protein

Protein 25g, Fat 4g, Carb 16g, Fibre 10g, 226 Kcals

Preparation

Put all the solid ingredients into the Tall Cup and press them down below the Max Line. Add the fluid base to fill the cup up to the Max Line. Screw the Nutribullet Extractor Blade on to the top of the cup. Invert the cup, press it down into the Nutribullet Power Base and twist it into place. Blast the mixture until it is really smooth (20 or so seconds). **Enjoy!**

Mint joins Papaya

Ingredients

2 Cups/Handfuls of Mint (80 grams or 3 oz)
¾ Cup of Papaya (90 grams or 3 oz)
1 Cup/Handful of Radishes (120 grams or 4 oz)
200 ml / 7 fl oz of Almond Milk (Unsweetened)
22 grams or ¾ oz of 85% Cocoa Chocolate

Protein 7g, Fat 14g, Carb 16g, Fibre 13g, 247 Kcals

Preparation

Put all the solid ingredients into the Tall Cup and press them down below the Max Line. Add the fluid base to fill the cup up to the Max Line. Screw the Nutribullet Extractor Blade on to the top of the cup. Invert the cup, press it down into the Nutribullet Power Base and twist it into place. Blast the mixture until it is really smooth (20 or so seconds). **Enjoy!**

Blackberry and Celery Surprise

Ingredients

2 Cups/Handfuls of Black Kale de-stemmed (80 grams or 3 oz)
¾ Cup of Blackberries (90 grams or 3 oz)
1 Cup/Handful of sliced Celery (120 grams or 4 oz)
200 ml / 7 fl oz of Hazelnut Milk
22 grams or ¾ oz of Ginger Root

Protein 6g, Fat 5g, Carb 16g, Fibre 10g, 161 Kcals

Preparation

Put all the solid ingredients into the Tall Cup and press them down below the Max Line. Add the fluid base to fill the cup up to the Max Line. Screw the Nutribullet Extractor Blade on to the top of the cup. Invert the cup, press it down into the Nutribullet Power Base and twist it into place. Blast the mixture until it is really smooth (20 or so seconds). **Enjoy!**

Lettuce and Cocoa Chocolate Royale

Ingredients

1 Cup/Handful of Lettuce Leaves (40 grams or 1½ oz)
1 Cup/Handful of Green Cabbage (40 grams or 1½ oz)
¾ Cup of Guava (90 grams or 3 oz)
1 Cup/Handful of sliced Asparagus (120 grams or 4 oz)
200 ml / 7 fl oz of Almond Milk (Unsweetened)
22 grams or ¾ oz of 85% Cocoa Chocolate

Protein 9g, Fat 14g, Carb 17g, Fibre 13g, 256 Kcals

Preparation

Put all the solid ingredients into the Tall Cup and press them down below the Max Line. Add the fluid base to fill the cup up to the Max Line. Screw the Nutribullet Extractor Blade on to the top of the cup. Invert the cup, press it down into the Nutribullet Power Base and twist it into place. Blast the mixture until it is really smooth (20 or so seconds). **Enjoy!**

Fennel meets Blackberry

Ingredients

1 Cup/Handful of Fennel (40 grams or 1½ oz)
1 Cup/Handful of Lettuce Leaves (40 grams or 1½ oz)
¾ Cup of Blackberries (90 grams or 3 oz)
1 Cup/Handful of sliced Green Pepper (120 grams or 4 oz)
200 ml / 7 fl oz of Coconut Milk
25 grams or 7/8 oz of Whey Protein (flavoured)

Protein 22g, Fat 5g, Carb 17g, Fibre 9g, 230 Kcals

Preparation

Put all the solid ingredients into the Tall Cup and press them down below the Max Line. Add the fluid base to fill the cup up to the Max Line. Screw the Nutribullet Extractor Blade on to the top of the cup. Invert the cup, press it down into the Nutribullet Power Base and twist it into place. Blast the mixture until it is really smooth (20 or so seconds). **Enjoy!**

Broccoli and Apricot Dance

Ingredients

1 Cup/Handful of Broccoli Florets (40 grams or 1½ oz)
1 Cup/Handful of Watercress (40 grams or 1½ oz)
¾ Cup of Apricot halves (90 grams or 3 oz)
1 Cup/Handful of sliced Red Pepper (120 grams or 4 oz)
200 ml / 7 fl oz of Almond Milk (Unsweetened)
25 grams or 7/8 oz of Whey Protein (flavoured)

Protein 24g, Fat 5g, Carb 17g, Fibre 6g, 233 Kcals

Preparation

Put all the solid ingredients into the Tall Cup and press them down below the Max Line. Add the fluid base to fill the cup up to the Max Line. Screw the Nutribullet Extractor Blade on to the top of the cup. Invert the cup, press it down into the Nutribullet Power Base and twist it into place. Blast the mixture until it is really smooth (20 or so seconds). **Enjoy!**

Black Kale and Raspberry Delight

Ingredients

2 Cups/Handfuls of Black Kale de-stemmed (80 grams or 3 oz)
¾ Cup of Raspberries (90 grams or 3 oz)
1 Cup/Handful of sliced Tomato (120 grams or 4 oz)
200 ml / 7 fl oz of Coconut Milk
25 grams or 7/8 oz of Pea Protein

Protein 25g, Fat 5g, Carb 18g, Fibre 9g, 238 Kcals

Preparation

Put all the solid ingredients into the Tall Cup and press them down below the Max Line. Add the fluid base to fill the cup up to the Max Line. Screw the Nutribullet Extractor Blade on to the top of the cup. Invert the cup, press it down into the Nutribullet Power Base and twist it into place. Blast the mixture until it is really smooth (20 or so seconds). *Enjoy!*

Strawberry and Fine Bean Pizzaz

Ingredients

1 Cup/Handful of Rocket/Arugura Lettuce (40 grams or 1½ oz)
1 Cup/Handful of Watercress (40 grams or 1½ oz)
¾ Cup of Strawberries (90 grams or 3 oz)
1 Cup/Handful of sliced Fine Beans (120 grams or 4 oz)
100 ml / 3½ fl oz of Almond Milk (Unsweetened)
100 ml / 3½ fl oz of Greek Yoghurt
25 grams or 7/8 oz of Pea Protein

Protein 28g, Fat 12g, Carb 18g, Fibre 6g, 308 Kcals

Preparation

Put all the solid ingredients into the Tall Cup and press them down below the Max Line. Add the fluid base to fill the cup up to the Max Line. Screw the Nutribullet Extractor Blade on to the top of the cup. Invert the cup, press it down into the Nutribullet Power Base and twist it into place. Blast the mixture until it is really smooth (20 or so seconds). *Enjoy!*

Lettuce and Avocado Sunshine

Ingredients

1 Cup/Handful of Spinach (40 grams or 1½ oz)
1 Cup/Handful of Lettuce Leaves (40 grams or 1½ oz)
¾ Cup of Avocado slices (90 grams or 3 oz)
1 Cup/Handful of sliced Fine Beans (120 grams or 4 oz)
200 ml / 7 fl oz of Dairy Milk Whole
25 grams or 7/8 oz of Rice Protein

Protein 32g, Fat 22g, Carb 18g, Fibre 10g, 411 Kcals

Preparation

Put all the solid ingredients into the Tall Cup and press them down below the Max Line. Add the fluid base to fill the cup up to the Max Line. Screw the Nutribullet Extractor Blade on to the top of the cup. Invert the cup, press it down into the Nutribullet Power Base and twist it into place. Blast the mixture until it is really smooth (20 or so seconds). **Enjoy!**

Orange and Spirulina Embrace

Ingredients

1 Cup/Handful of Black Kale de-stemmed (40 grams or 1½ oz)
1 Cup/Handful of Watercress (40 grams or 1½ oz)
¾ Cup of Orange segments (90 grams or 3 oz)
1 Cup/Handful of diced Turnip (120 grams or 4 oz)
200 ml / 7 fl oz of Almond Milk (Unsweetened)
15 grams or ½ oz of Spirulina

Protein 14g, Fat 4g, Carb 19g, Fibre 6g, 162 Kcals

Preparation

Put all the solid ingredients into the Tall Cup and press them down below the Max Line. Add the fluid base to fill the cup up to the Max Line. Screw the Nutribullet Extractor Blade on to the top of the cup. Invert the cup, press it down into the Nutribullet Power Base and twist it into place. Blast the mixture until it is really smooth (20 or so seconds). **Enjoy!**

Veggie Wonder

Ingredients

1 Cup/Handful of Spinach (40 grams or 1½ oz)
1 Cup/Handful of Rocket/Arugura Lettuce (40 grams or 1½ oz)
¾ Cup of Papaya (90 grams or 3 oz)
1 Cup/Handful of sliced Celery (120 grams or 4 oz)
100 ml / 3½ fl oz of Almond Milk (Unsweetened)
100 ml / 3½ fl oz of Greek Yoghurt
25 grams or 7/8 oz of Whey Protein (flavoured)

Protein 27g, Fat 13g, Carb 19g, Fibre 5g, 320 Kcals

Preparation

Put all the solid ingredients into the Tall Cup and press them down below the Max Line. Add the fluid base to fill the cup up to the Max Line. Screw the Nutribullet Extractor Blade on to the top of the cup. Invert the cup, press it down into the Nutribullet Power Base and twist it into place. Blast the mixture until it is really smooth (20 or so seconds). **Enjoy!**

Orange and Turnip Concerto

Ingredients

2 Cups/Handfuls of Green Cabbage (80 grams or 3 oz)
¾ Cup of Orange segments (90 grams or 3 oz)
1 Cup/Handful of diced Turnip (120 grams or 4 oz)
200 ml / 7 fl oz of Almond Milk (Unsweetened)
25 grams or 7/8 oz of Whey Protein (flavoured)

Protein 23g, Fat 4g, Carb 19g, Fibre 7g, 230 Kcals

Preparation

Put all the solid ingredients into the Tall Cup and press them down below the Max Line. Add the fluid base to fill the cup up to the Max Line. Screw the Nutribullet Extractor Blade on to the top of the cup. Invert the cup, press it down into the Nutribullet Power Base and twist it into place. Blast the mixture until it is really smooth (20 or so seconds). **Enjoy!**

Bok Choy on Water Melon

Ingredients

1 Cup/Handful of Green Cabbage (40 grams or 1½ oz)
1 Cup/Handful of Bok Choy (40 grams or 1½ oz)
¾ Cup of Water Melon chunks (90 grams or 3 oz)
1 Cup/Handful of sliced Zucchini/Courgette (120 grams or 4 oz)
200 ml / 7 fl oz of Hazelnut Milk
25 grams or 7/8 oz of Rice Protein

Protein 24g, Fat 4g, Carb 19g, Fibre 4g, 213 Kcals

Preparation

Put all the solid ingredients into the Tall Cup and press them down below the Max Line. Add the fluid base to fill the cup up to the Max Line. Screw the Nutribullet Extractor Blade on to the top of the cup. Invert the cup, press it down into the Nutribullet Power Base and twist it into place. Blast the mixture until it is really smooth (20 or so seconds). **Enjoy!**

Rocket and Peach Refrain

Ingredients

2 Cups/Handfuls of Rocket/Arugura Lettuce (80 grams or 3 oz)
¾ Cup of Peach slices (90 grams or 3 oz)
1 Cup/Handful of sliced Cauliflower florets (120 grams or 4 oz)
200 ml / 7 fl oz of Hazelnut Milk
25 grams or 7/8 oz of Whey Protein (unflavoured)

Protein 25g, Fat 6g, Carb 19g, Fibre 5g, 235 Kcals

Preparation

Put all the solid ingredients into the Tall Cup and press them down below the Max Line. Add the fluid base to fill the cup up to the Max Line. Screw the Nutribullet Extractor Blade on to the top of the cup. Invert the cup, press it down into the Nutribullet Power Base and twist it into place. Blast the mixture until it is really smooth (20 or so seconds). **Enjoy!**

Rocket embraces Blackberry

Ingredients

1 Cup/Handful of Rocket/Arugura Lettuce (40 grams or 1½ oz)
1 Cup/Handful of Broccoli Florets (40 grams or 1½ oz)
¾ Cup of Blackberries (90 grams or 3 oz)
1 Cup/Handful of sliced Red Pepper (120 grams or 4 oz)
200 ml / 7 fl oz of Hazelnut Milk
15 grams or ½ oz of Chlorella

Protein 12g, Fat 6g, Carb 19g, Fibre 9g, 207 Kcals

Preparation

Put all the solid ingredients into the Tall Cup and press them down below the Max Line. Add the fluid base to fill the cup up to the Max Line. Screw the Nutribullet Extractor Blade on to the top of the cup. Invert the cup, press it down into the Nutribullet Power Base and twist it into place. Blast the mixture until it is really smooth (20 or so seconds). *Enjoy!*

Grapefruit loves Carrot

Ingredients

1 Cup/Handful of Rocket/Arugura Lettuce (40 grams or 1½ oz)
1 Cup/Handful of Spinach (40 grams or 1½ oz)
¾ Cup of Grapefruit segments (90 grams or 3 oz)
1 Cup/Handful of sliced Carrots (120 grams or 4 oz)
200 ml / 7 fl oz of Almond Milk (Unsweetened)
15 grams or ½ oz of Spirulina

Protein 13g, Fat 4g, Carb 19g, Fibre 7g, 161 Kcals

Preparation

Put all the solid ingredients into the Tall Cup and press them down below the Max Line. Add the fluid base to fill the cup up to the Max Line. Screw the Nutribullet Extractor Blade on to the top of the cup. Invert the cup, press it down into the Nutribullet Power Base and twist it into place. Blast the mixture until it is really smooth (20 or so seconds). *Enjoy!*

Avocado and Red Pepper Journey

Ingredients

1 Cup/Handful of Black Kale de-stemmed (40 grams or 1½ oz)
1 Cup/Handful of Bok Choy (40 grams or 1½ oz)
¾ Cup of Avocado slices (90 grams or 3 oz)
1 Cup/Handful of sliced Red Pepper (120 grams or 4 oz)
200 ml / 7 fl oz of Dairy Milk Whole
25 grams or 7/8 oz of Rice Protein

Protein 31g, Fat 22g, Carb 19g, Fibre 10g, 421 Kcals

Preparation

Put all the solid ingredients into the Tall Cup and press them down below the Max Line. Add the fluid base to fill the cup up to the Max Line. Screw the Nutribullet Extractor Blade on to the top of the cup. Invert the cup, press it down into the Nutribullet Power Base and twist it into place. Blast the mixture until it is really smooth (20 or so seconds). *Enjoy!*

NOTES

10723930R00072

Printed in Great Britain
by Amazon.co.uk, Ltd.,
Marston Gate.